Making Your Website Work:
100 Copy & Design Tweaks for Smart Business Owners

Gill Andrews

Table of Contents

Below, you'll find the titles of all 100 chapters listed one by one. If you'd like a more compact overview of the topics this book covers, use the Index at the end that organizes the content by topics.

Introduction

When I was nine or ten, I saw a movie about a girl from another planet who gets stuck on Earth.

At some point, she has to go to school. Everyone knows she's an alien, but her classmates are still surprised when she tells them that on her planet, if you want to learn something new, they just give you an injection and – bam! – you're an expert.

"Wow", I thought to myself. "I want that, too!"

I've been waiting for a 'knowledge shot' to get invented ever since, terribly missing it during the chemistry lessons at high school – a subject I wouldn't be able to grasp even if my life depended on it.

But alas. We carry a whole library in our pockets and our vacuum cleaner can send us text messages, yet we still have to learn stuff by actually studying it.

"Learning is easy when it's fun", says an inspirational quote on Pinterest. And it's not wrong. But even fun learning is a burden if one feels guilty spending time on it or if that newly acquired knowledge doesn't make any difference in one's life.

Take you, for example.

You want to learn how to make your website earn you more money (if you don't, this is awkward; I hope you didn't draw anything in this book and can still return it to where you got it from).

More money is one hell of a motivation, but when you have a business to run and a life to manage, taking a course or reading a pile of books seem impossible to fit into your schedule.

You can't even finish reading the blog posts you find online! Although I don't blame you. Many of them are boring, vague or both, leaving you with more questions than answers.

Well, I have some good news and some bad news for you.

First, the bad news.

You have no choice.

Whether you take care of your website yourself or hire people to do it for you, as a smart business owner you can't afford not to understand what makes web copy effective, how to spot bad design or what mistakes to avoid in your website structure.

Otherwise, you risk spending years wondering why you don't get enough business through your website, even after you've paid others a lot of money to beautify it.

The good news is that you don't have to take a long course or bury yourself in books for a year to understand what makes a website work and what doesn't.

You can learn it from this very book you're holding in your hands.

It doesn't teach you all the copywriting formulas or make you learn design rules by heart.

Instead, it describes real website problems that freelancers, digital agencies, ecommerce shops and SaaS companies face – the same problems you have with your website – and shows you how to fix them.

You'll learn how to spot (and fix) vague and self-centered copy, how to sound trustworthy even without testimonials or what phrases to avoid not to sound condescending.

You'll learn how to spot sloppy web design, how many call-to-action buttons to put on your homepage and why you should kill your drop-down menus.

You'll learn many practical things you can implement on your website right away, and you'll learn all of that without feeling overwhelmed.

Every chapter in this book is about 200 words – a snack of knowledge you can take once a day, or any time you feel like it, that will help you improve your website bit by bit and make you better prepared for many website challenges to come.

Before we dive in

To clarify: The truly accurate answer to every website-related question out there is "it depends".

Whether and how to change something on *your* website depends on your target audience, your business model and a dozen of other things that make your website and your business situation unique. Which makes it almost impossible to give you 100% accurate advice without looking at your website first.

So, you shouldn't view the tips in this book as one-size-fits-all solutions but rather the safe choices in the majority of cases.

Every tip comes with a rational explanation of the advice given based on the principles one should be guided by when creating a business website: clarity, value, relevancy and minimal distractions and friction.

The arguments that come with each tip will allow you to make an informed decision as to whether a particular piece of advice is something that, if applied to your website, will improve it.

Who is this book for?

This book is for **business owners who take care of their website themselves** – write their own copy and create their own web pages. You'll learn how to write better copy and how to make sure that your design doesn't kill your message (or, at least, doesn't get in the way).

This book is for **copywriters** who want to sharpen their skill and also learn how to prevent designers from murdering their copy later on. You'll learn to spot bad design decisions and discover powerful arguments to use in conversations with your clients and their designers.

Plus, you'll get to charge more for your services, because after you've read this book, you'll have a better understanding of what makes design convert (and what doesn't).

This book is for **web designers** who want to design not only pretty websites but also websites that convert. You'll learn to distinguish bad copy from good copy to be able to warn your clients in advance that their copy has problems (or, at least, not to be the one to get blamed for the low conversion rate once the website is live).

This book is also for **business owners who are planning to hire someone** to create their website for them. You'll learn how to spot ineffective copy and sloppy design to make sure that the pretty website you're paying for will also convert.

How to use this book

What's your favorite number? You can start with that tip number. Or do the even numbers first. Or the primes.

The order in which you read the tips doesn't matter, but if there are some topics that interest you more than others, pay attention to the icons before each tip.

 Blogging: Tips that help you get more people to read your blog posts. Many web design or strategy tips can also be applied to your blog pages, of course. But the ones marked with "B" focus specifically on blogs.

 Copywriting: Tips that help you create engaging copy that sells your offers for you and / or avoid copy mistakes that drive your prospects away.

 Web design: Tips that show you how to make sure your web design is making your message stronger (or, at least, isn't getting in the way).

 Strategy: Tips that help you be strategic with the changes you make to your website to keep people on it for longer, to get more subscribers, to cater to the different segments of your audience better, and so on.

 User experience: Tips that help you make it easy for your prospects to find what they're looking for on your website and complete their tasks without frustration or confusion.

At the end of the book, you'll also find an **index** that matches different topics to the book pages to help you find relevant tips faster.

Glossary

To make sure we're on the same page, here are some terms used in this book and their meanings.

A/B testing: A way to compare two almost identical versions of a web page with one thing being different to find out which version of the page performs better with respect to a particular metric (number of clicks on a certain link, sign-ups, sales, etc.)

Above the fold area: The part of your page visible to your website visitors right after they opened it before they scroll down.

Call to action (CTA): A button or a link that asks your website visitors to do something ("Sign up", "Contact me", etc.) that usually leads your prospects further down the sales funnel.

Conversion: A conversion occurs when a website visitor takes an action you wanted them to take (for example, signs up for your newsletter or buys your product).

Friction: Anything that slows down your prospect while they're exploring your website. Bad friction is a pointless hurdle that may irritate your prospects (too many visual highlights, extensive animations, etc.). Good friction makes your prospects pay attention to important things (bold heading that indicates a start of a new section, visually prominent call-to-action button, etc.).

Features vs benefits: A feature is what a product does (for example, moisturizes one's skin) or contains (for example, two on-demand videos), or what a service includes (for example, 30-min website audit). A benefit is how your product or service will improve the lives of your prospects (for example, makes them feel younger, helps them close more deals, helps them sell more through their websites).

Heading: A phrase on a web page highlighted in bold that indicates a start of a new section and tells your prospects what it will be about. It can also refer to a section in a sidebar or a footer.

Interstitial: Pop-ups or full-screen overlays that appear on top of the content of the page you're currently reading and usually contain a sign-up form or an ad.

Lead magnet: A resource (ebook, checklist, quiz results, etc.) that potential clients who visit your website (aka "leads") can download for free in exchange for their email address.

Opt-in: A form that lets prospects sign up for something with an email address (for example, to receive a free ebook, to sign up for a webinar, to sign up for a newsletter).

Sales funnel: A path your prospects take from the moment they hear about you for the first time to the moment they buy your product or service. Here's an example of a sales funnel: Clicked on a tweet => read your latest blog post => signed up for a lead magnet => engaged with your emails => clicked on a link in the promo email => signed up for your paid course.

Screen view: The part of your page a website visitor sees on their screen at once.

Social proof: Generally speaking, this is a psychological and social phenomenon where people look at the behavior of others to decide how they should behave in a situation themselves, especially when feeling uncertain. On your website, social proof manifests itself through testimonials, case studies, your certificates, awards, features in famous publications, etc.

Subtagline: A sentence or a short paragraph right after the website tagline.

Unique value proposition (UVP): A clear statement that tells your prospects what you do, how you solve your customers' problems and why they should choose you and not your competitors. Also known as "unique selling point (USP)".

Website tagline: The first sentence or phrase your website visitors see above the fold when they land on your homepage.

#1: Why you shouldn't welcome your visitors on your website

"Welcome to my website! I'm happy you stopped by!"

Phew. Glad we clarified that because your visitors already started to think you really don't want them there.

Joking aside, the time people are willing to spend on your website is limited. Not only might they get bored with irrelevant info or jargon (things you can control), but they also might get interrupted by a phone call, a train stop where they need to get off, or a kid asking for a snack (things you can't control, aka "life").

That's why you need to make every second count. Everything on your website – every word, every button, every image – needs to have a purpose.

This purpose can be different: to entertain, to inform, to spark an emotion, to prompt an action, etc. But if you have elements and text with no purpose, you're wasting people's time and your own money.

It's especially true for meaningless text, such as:

1) Things that are implied, like "Welcome to my website", "I invite you to look around", etc.

Want your visitors to feel welcome? Value their time and offer them relevant information right away.

Want to invite them to look around? Make it easy to browse your website and use clear navigation.

2) Things that don't mean anything concrete.

Your visitors can't imagine anything concrete when they read things like "high-impact solution", "results driven" or "digital space".

Want to inform? Use words that are specific enough to create a clear picture in your visitors' minds. Because if they can't imagine it, they won't buy it.

#2: Six questions that will expose the main flaws of your website

This is a true story of how asking the right questions cost me the job.

A small business owner wanted me to review her website. We agreed on the fees, and she asked me to send her the contract.

Together with a contract, I sent her a questionnaire I always send before I review a website to learn more about her business and target audience.

After a couple of days, she emailed me saying that she'd decided to change her business strategy and will be changing the website, too. So, a review right now won't make sense.

I wasn't surprised. Her website was a mess, and I can imagine that after reading my questions she saw why.

So, what questions exposed the flaws of a website without a review? Here are some of them:

1) Could you please explain your offer in a couple of sentences?

2) What is your unique value proposition? Why should someone hire you and not your competitor?

3) Who is your ideal client?

4) What is your strategy for getting new clients through your website?

5) What is your current monthly traffic and your main traffic sources?

6) Who are your competitors? BHA

Can you answer all these questions confidently? Are you still happy with your website and the way you've structured your offers?

P.S. Needless to say, I now send that questionnaire only after a contract has been signed.

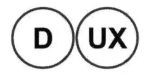

#3: Unless you're an amusement park, there shouldn't be any carousels on your website

"But I really like how my slider looks!", wrote my client to me after I reviewed his website and told him to kill that carousel in the homepage header.

I understand. I like how it looks too, Greg. But that's the only good thing about it.

Fact, proven by numerous case studies:

Sliders, aka "carousels", aren't effective in communicating important stuff (or getting people to click on them, for that matter). They rotate faster than your prospects are able to absorb the info.

Homepage header carousels. Client logo carousels. Testimonial carousels.

They have no place on an efficient website, because self-moving elements ~~drive your visitors crazy~~ harm the user experience:

- Animated post carousels usually result in fewer clicks.

- Testimonial carousels don't give your visitors enough time to read.

- Client logos that fly in and out keep your visitors from reading further, while they stare at your moving logos wondering whether there's more to come.

- Your visitors are likely to ignore the moving elements because they automatically assume they're ads.

- It's just plain annoying for your website visitors to lose control of the user interface when things move around by themselves.

"But <insert a famous website here> uses a slider in its header!"

Sure, but the company that owns this website:

- Is famous (and you aren't) and has many repeated visitors who already know their value proposition (and you don't)

- Has A/B tested that slider and has statistical proof that it's better than a static image with text (have you?)

Want a slider on your website? A/B test it. Or, at least, become famous.

#4: Don't tell your visitors how to feel

I still remember this embarrassing moment as if it were yesterday.

We were practicing our dance moves for a concert in high school. I decided to remember my ballet past and did what was supposed to be a *grand jeté* (a split jump).

As the last time I did ballet was ten years ago at that point, my jump had the grace of a hippopotamus jumping over a puddle.

I was well aware of this but decided to play it cool. "Awesome, huh?", I said to the teacher supervising the practice.

#awkwardsilence

Easy, isn't it?

Isn't it great?

How awesome is that?

This is you making your prospects feel awkward if they don't share your sentiment. And although it's great when your copy evokes emotions, 'awkward', 'patronized' or 'talked down to' is not what you want your prospects to feel.

Want your prospects to feel excited about your offer? Don't tell them how to feel.

Instead, tell them:

- How your offer solves their problems by phrasing features through benefits

- How it makes their lives better by painting the picture of their lives after they buy it

- What your customers / clients think about you / your product by including credible testimonials

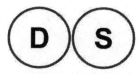

#5: Want people to stay longer on your website? Start with a clear homepage

Many of your website visitors don't know what you do. They're checking out your homepage to learn more about you and your offer.

But if you greet them with:

- a cryptic website tagline
- walls of text
- countless images and links that pull their attention in all possible directions
- no or unclear calls to action

... they'll close the browser tab faster than you can blink.

Want people to stay longer on your website? Start with a clear homepage.

1) State your name / the name of your company. If you are a one-person brand, place your photograph prominently on your homepage.

2) Tell your visitors what you do, what you offer and what's in it for them clearly, using words you're 100% sure your target audience understands.

3) Define your homepage goals. What would be an ideal action for your visitors to take on your homepage (subscribe to your email list, check out your Services page, contact you, etc.)?

4) Based on your goals, remove everything that pulls their attention in the wrong direction.

5) Add more information that may increase the chances of them taking that action (testimonials, quotes from your case studies, videos, etc.).

6) Add clear calls to action to tell people what they should do next.

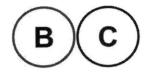

#6: Get to the point quickly or risk losing a reader

You've experienced this before.

You're looking for a recipe for homemade hummus. You click on a link, but before you can get to the instructions, you have to scroll down for two miles through "What is hummus?", "Who invented hummus?" and "28 types of hummus North African Bedouins want you to taste".

You get frustrated, order pizza, and go off to write a "10 copywriting tips" blog post... following the same pattern. Instead of telling people what your headline promised right away, you make them suffer through numerous sections of irrelevant blah blah.

Why?

You may be doing it for two reasons.

Reason #1: Everyone's doing it.

Oh, come on! Don't you think it's a bad idea to copy something not knowing the exact reason behind it?

Reason #2: SEO.

It's a tactic some blogs use to rank for the queries of "What is..." with the posts that are actually about a narrower topic. This way they can use their keyword more often, which should be better for ranking.

But Google constantly updates its algorithm. And although you can't predict the algorithm changes, one thing is for sure: it will follow the user's needs.

So, in the long run, you're better off giving your readers what they want. And what they want is for you to get to the point quickly.

Get to the point quickly, or you risk losing a reader

10 Copywriting Tips

What is copywriting?

Why copy is important?

Tip #1

Tip #1

Tip #2

Tip #3

#7: Stages of awareness and what your prospects need to hear in each of them

A prospect on your Contact page doesn't need to hear about the benefits of your offer. She's heard enough and now just wants an easy way to get in touch.

A seasoned businessman doesn't need to read five paragraphs describing his problems. He wants to know if you can solve them.

Defining your audience doesn't end with age, gender or occupation. For every page, think about:

- What do they know about their situation and your offer?
- What's missing for them to convert?

First described by Eugene Schwartz in his book "Breakthrough Advertising", the first question has five possible answers, which he calls "stages of customer awareness".

Here's what you need to tell different prospects with different awareness levels for them to give you their money.

Stage #1: Completely unaware

These prospects don't know anything about your offer / problems you solve.

=> Start by speaking to their state of mind.

Stage #2: Problem-aware

These prospects are aware of their problems but don't know how to solve them or even that a solution exists.

=> Start by showing them that you understand their pain and present them the 'what' of your solution.

Stage #3: Solution-aware

These prospects know what result they want but don't know that your solution can help them achieve it.

=> Show them how and why your solution works and explain its benefits.

Stage #4: Product-aware

These prospects know what you sell but aren't sure it's right for them.

=> Tell them how your solution is different and prove that it works.

Stage #5: Most aware

These prospects know their problems, the result they want and that your product helps. They just want to see the deal.

=> Show them the deal right away.

#8: Hide your "follow me" social icons

"Follow me" social icons that take your visitors to your Twitter, Facebook or Pinterest profile have no place in your website header.

Nor in your sidebar.

Nor anywhere else where your visitors might click on them before they see the rest of the page.

Your visitors have just come to your website, and you should do everything possible to keep them there.

If you give them a chance to leave by showing them those shiny "follow me" icons, they might take it and never come back.

Sure, at first they'll land on your social profile, but then you'll lose them to baby pictures, cat memes and cake recipes.

The best place for the "follow me" social icons on your website?

Your website footer.

If someone genuinely wants to follow you on social media, they'll scroll down to find those links. Everyone else should stay on your website and explore more of your content.

Bonus tip: Make sure you include only the links to the social networks you regularly post on (unless you're equally active on Twitter, Facebook, Pinterest, LinkedIn and Instagram).

#9: Delete your Testimonials page

Do you have a Testimonials page? If you do, check your Google Analytics reports to see how many people visit it. I bet there aren't many.

But that's not your biggest problem.

Every testimonial is more powerful in context, next to a claim you want your prospects to believe, and not in a pile of ten other testimonials on your Testimonials page that your prospects may or may not discover.

Want to persuade more website visitors to take action? Add client testimonials where they matter – on your homepage, About, service and product pages, and anywhere else where you want your prospects to take the next step.

Only use effective testimonials that:

- Are short and direct
- Use full names and, if possible, headshots
- Are specific enough to sound authentic
- Do at least one of these three things:
    - Reinforce your unique value proposition
    - Use data behind the value your service or product delivers
    - Address initial fears of your customers and explain how they were eliminated
- If possible, contain the keyword you've optimized that page for

Anatomy of an effective testimonial

"Better leads, 35% increase in sign-ups" ◄ Main takeaway

We hired John to rewrite our homepage that didn't reflect our value proposition anymore and was barely bringing us leads. We noticed an improvement in lead quality almost immediately after the page went live. The sign-up rate for our free trial is also up 35%. We couldn't be happier with John and his work.

What was done

Specific benefits

Rick Miller, CEO, FlyChart

Name / company

#10: Don't make your headings look like buttons

When someone lands on your page, they first skim through. They pause and start reading only when something catches their eye.

It can be difficult for visitors to skim your page when you direct their attention to the wrong elements or clutter the page with too many things at once.

For example, when your headings look like buttons.

If you use this style for the widget titles in the sidebar or have many headings on your page, the color backgrounds make your page cluttered.

Help your visitors find relevant spots and dive into your content faster by reducing clutter and making all elements look like they function.

Non-clickable text should look like plain text:

- No distinct font color
- No background color
- Not underlined

For headings: Use a different font family, bigger and / or capitalized letters.

Links should look clickable:

- Within articles: Distinct color and underlined, or distinct color and underlined on hover
- As calls to action: "Button look" – contrast background color, color change on hover (optional)

This will save your visitors mental energy and time, and they'll thank you for it by staying on your page longer.

Don't make your headings look like buttons

Want this benefit?

Learn More

Want this benefit?

Learn More

22

#11: Nobody's clicking on your CTA button? Try this

So, you use a free ebook to grow your list. Or maybe you're trying to get more people to sign up for your webinar.

Where have you placed that sign-up button?

Is it at the top of the page, shining with bright colors? Or did you bury it within your content and made it look only slightly different from the rest of your page?

"Duh, Gill, of course I made it clearly visible! You know, with bright colors and featured box and stuff".

I see.

What if I told you that more people may click on your button if you bury it deeper down the page and make it less visually prominent?

Your CTA button is asking people for a commitment. But what if you haven't given them enough information to make a decision yet?

Tell them more about your thing before asking them to click that button, and more people may do that.

Your visitors may also be 'banner blind'. Bombarded by thousands of ads daily, they've learned to ignore parts of your web page that look like ads.

So, what would be a better way to get their attention? You guessed it. Don't make that content block that promotes your ebook look like an ad.

#12: Don't overuse one-line paragraphs

Are you using one-line paragraphs on your website?

Ah, these trendy one-liners!

The breath of fresh air.

The cold pack for the eye.

In your face, every English language teacher out there!

I say let's write in one-line paragraphs only.

Just kidding, of course.

Let's not.

Here's why.

To keep your visitors reading, you need to make sure they don't get visually bored. And after poor readability, visual monotony is your archenemy #2.

The original purpose of one-line paragraphs is to bring novelty into the reading experience and to break the monotony of longer paragraphs.

But guess what happens if you use more than three one-liners immediately after each other? Right, it stops being new and becomes monotonous again.

To make people read more of your content, don't use too many consecutive one-liners.

Instead, vary the length of your paragraphs between 4-, 3-, 2- and 1-liners to avoid visually boring your visitors.

#13: When using text on an image, make sure the text remains readable

This is often the case with header images on homepages and featured images of blog posts:

- The background image is too busy.

- The text color doesn't have enough contrast => The text is hard to read => Your website visitors start to silently curse you.

When using an image as a background for text, ask yourself:

Is it reeeally necessary to use an image or could you use a plain color background instead?

If you must use an image as a background:

- Place the text on the part where the image is less busy

- Select a font color that stands out from the rest of the image

- Consider using a semi-transparent background behind the text (see the example on the next page)

Make sure the text on your images is readable

This is better
Much better

This is unreadable
and so is this

#14: How to discover (and eliminate) self-centered copy on your website

We all have a friend who just won't shut up about themselves.

Every time you talk to them, it's "me, me, me". So annoying! You wish for the conversation to be over before it even started.

Well, I've got news for you: This is how your prospects feel about you if your copy is self-centered.

If you:

- use "I" / "we" in your copy more often than "you"

- describe the features of your product or service without mentioning the benefits

- ramble on about your journey and life philosophy on your About page

... your copy is self-centered.

But most of your visitors who aren't your mom care only about what you can do for them. So, you need to center your copy around their needs if you want them to pay attention.

Here's how to tell if you're talking too much about yourself:

1) Open a page on your website.

2) Press Ctrl+F and type "I " (remember the space character after "I").

3) Write down the number of occurrences.

4) Repeat for "my", "you", "your" and compare the numbers.

- If you used "I" / "my" more often than "you" / "your", rephrase the self-centered sentences:

  o Business owners, users, individuals => You

- I'll provide => You'll get

- I'll teach => You'll learn

- I'll show you how => Find out how

- I work with one client at a time => Your project will have my undivided attention

And here's how to better address your customers' needs in your copy:

- Make sure your website tagline and subtagline focus on how you can solve your customers' problems.

- Describe your services or the features of your products using benefits.

- Don't bore your prospects with never-ending stories about your childhood, hobbies or career on your About page. Instead, tell them more about why you do what you do and why they should trust you.

- Describe the ways you can help your potential customers solve their problems and focus on building trust, regardless of the page.

Forget pretty photos and expensive design themes. Instead, make this simple change to your copy to instantly connect with your visitors.

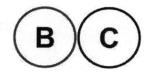

#15: Not getting enough client inquiries? Make your service pages longer

Your service pages don't perform well? Your prospects may need more details to feel confident enough that you and your services are the right fit.

Add more text to your individual service pages explaining to your prospects:

- What happens after they contact you

- How you're going to deliver that service (i.e. your process)

- Why they can be certain you'll do a good job by including social proof (case studies, testimonials, etc.)

- What happens if they aren't happy with the outcome

- How much you charge

To state or not to state your fees, that is the question. The only way to find out the answer is to test it for your own website and business.

If you don't give any numbers on your service pages and you don't get enough inquiries or get too many irrelevant ones, try stating your fees and see what happens.

#16: Three things to keep in mind when using images on your website

With words, you can make sure that all your prospects understand and feel the same way about what you're saying.

Images, on the other hand, are much more likely to get misinterpreted or to trigger an undesired emotion.

Keep these three things in mind when selecting images for your website to make sure they don't undermine your message.

1) Will it always evoke a positive emotion?

Let's say you call yourself "Word Doctor" and want to have an image of a doctor on your website. A risky move, as most people's subconscience freaks out when they see anything that reminds them of a hospital.

This is an extreme example, but it can happen with more innocent topics as well. So, make sure any image you use *always* evokes an emotion that will help you sell.

2) Is the meaning clear?

Let's say you're using a fallen chess queen next to the copy that talks about winning. But the image can also mean "losing". So, its meaning isn't 100% clear.

Make sure your image can't be misinterpreted.

3) Does it match your color palette?

This isn't as important for any images used further down the page as it is for a featured image visible on top of the article where it's surrounded by other colors (navigation, author's photo, links, etc.).

If it has a dominant color that clashes with the main colors of your theme, your visitors may feel irritated, which will overshadow the positive first impression you were hoping to make.

Will it always evoke a positive emotion?

Does it match your color palette?

Is the meaning clear?

Using images on your website

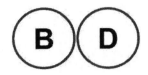

#17: This is the main killer of your business message on your website

Visual clutter.

The more text columns, images and CTA buttons that are competing for your visitors' attention, the less attention each of them receives.

Also, if your page is visually cluttered, your visitors won't be able to recognize what's important and may not take the action you want them to take.

To beat visual clutter:

- Use enough white space
- Use fewer highlights and colors
- Avoid having too many color-rich elements on one screen view
- Use consistent styling of headings, subheadings, widget titles, etc.
- Maintain visual hierarchy to communicate the relative importance of the elements:
  - Make what's important visually prominent
  - Make logically related elements also visually related

#18: Don't make your homepage about you

You may well think, *"What else did my visitors come to my homepage for other than to learn about me?"*

Yet, most visitors don't care about you. They care about what you can do for them. So, a homepage that focuses on how awesome you are or your "values and philosophy" is a big turnoff.

The only two things on your homepage that should be about you are:

- Your name / your company's name
- Your photograph / photos of your team members

The rest – even that website tagline and the part where you describe your products or services – should be about how you can help.

For every line of text on your website, ask yourself:

"How can I phrase it to show the benefit of working with me / buying my product?"

Here are a couple of ideas:

- What's that one main problem that you help people solve? Make this sentence your tagline.
- Rephrase features through benefits.
- Make sure the titles of your posts reflect the benefits people will get from reading them.
- Use an opt-in form to capture email addresses, instead of just saying "Sign up for updates". Add a line explaining what your prospects can expect from your updates and promise a benefit.

#19: How many CTA buttons should you put on your homepage?

"You should always design your pages around one call to action."

If you've heard (and followed) this piece of advice before, I'm here to tell you to forget it.

Sure, some pages should be designed around one call to action. But some pages definitely shouldn't, and your homepage is one of them.

Why?

Because you can't predict where a visitor who lands on your homepage came from or what she wants.

Has she found you through search or from a post on social media?

Has she heard of you before, is she ready to hire you, or is she just looking around?

So, you need to anticipate the needs of the different segments of your target audience and show each of them the way to the relevant pages.

To do that, you need multiple sections and CTA buttons on your homepage.

Here's how to decide what they should be (see also the image at the end of this chapter).

Step #1: Brainstorm the possible CTAs.

Step #2: Color-code the CTAs (for example, red, yellow and green) based on how difficult you think it will be to persuade your visitors to take that action (i.e. based on the level of commitment).

Step #3: Arrange your CTAs from top to bottom based on how valuable a click on that CTA is to you.

Step #4: Decide what CTAs to keep based on the following rules of thumb:

- No more than one CTA button should be visible simultaneously on one screen view (unless it's products or services CTAs).

- The higher the level of commitment that an action requires, the more compelling your copy needs to be.

Need a real-life example of how to use this process? You'll find it in an article on my website Gillandrews.com called *"How Many CTA Buttons Should You Put on Your Homepage?"*.

Calls to Action

Value for your business

very valuable ← less valuable

- Contact me
- Register for my course
- Download free ebook
- Check out case studies
- Check out services
- Check out About page
- Read latest blog posts

■ - high commitment

▨ - medium commitment

⬚ - low commitment

#20: Your copy can only communicate your message clearly if your design isn't in the way

Did you know that your visitors form their first opinion about your website within about 50 milliseconds? To add insult to injury, 94% of that opinion is design related.

Even if you have brilliant copy that is:

- clear
- customer focused
- free of jargon, buzzwords and superlatives,

... it won't be effective if you have:

- visual clutter
- misaligned elements
- poor text formatting
- walls of text
- too many highlights
- annoying pop-ups

These things not only hide the important part of your message but can also communicate something totally different:

"I'm an amateur. I don't know what I'm doing. I can't be trusted."

Is this your business message? I hope not.

So, before making a design decision for your website, ask yourself:

- Why do I want this element or feature on my page: Because it makes my message stronger or because it looks fancy?

- What did my visitors come to this page for?

- Is this element or feature pulling my visitors' attention in the wrong direction?

- Will this thing annoy them or interrupt their train of thought?

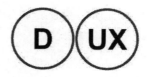

#21: Have a drop-down menu in your navigation? Kill it with fire!

Here's something counter-intuitive: Your visitors don't like your drop-down menus.

- They find them annoying and irritating.

- They tend to skip top-level pages.

- Drop-down menus make it harder to find things.

- You may have created thin content – pages with so little content that neither your prospects nor the search engines will consider it valuable.

This holds for drop-down menus of all sizes, not only the long ones.

Here are four alternatives to a drop-down menu that will make navigating your website a breeze (and keep people on your website longer):

1) Have only one drop-down item? Either put it as a top-level navigation item or remove it from the navigation altogether.

2) Have a drop-down under "About"? Combine the info from all these pages on one About page.

3) Have a drop-down under Services? Create a dedicated Services landing page that has several paragraphs and CTA buttons featuring separate services and leading your prospects to the respective pages.

   Exception: If you have three to five services with very clear and distinct titles that need no explanation for your visitor to make a choice.

4) If you feel you need a crazy long drop-down, use a mega menu (you know, the two-dimensional menus typical for online retailer websites).

#22: Your website doesn't need to have beautiful design to be effective

Do you often look at beautiful websites and feel jealous because your website isn't that pretty?

Good news: Your visitors don't care if your website has awesome design. On the contrary, many websites that look beautiful at first glance are difficult to use because their design gets in the way.

Your website theme and design don't need to be beautiful. Not ugly but functional is more than enough.

Your web design is great if:

- it helps your visitors do what they came to your website for, and
- it helps you convert them.

Don't aim for entertaining your visitors with fancy features. Rather, design your website in a way that doesn't interfere with what people came to your website for.

Make sure that your web pages:

- Load fast
- Are free of clutter
- Make everything easy to read
- Use proper visual hierarchy
- Are free of distractions

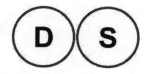

#23: Don't neglect your website footer

A footer seems to be the most underestimated part of a business website. Which is ironic, because it's an area your visitors see on every page.

This makes the footer ideal for drawing attention to important information, pages or products, keeping your visitors longer on your website and helping them navigate it.

Here are some things you can include in your footer:

- A snippet about you / your company (+ your photo)
- Navigation to main pages
- Latest articles
- Call to action
- Email sign-up
- Search box
- Contact information
- Postal address / link to a map
- Social icons
- Copyright
- Privacy policy
- Terms of use

Not all of these points have to be in your footer, of course. A cluttered footer is as bad as an empty one. Just select the most relevant for you and your business.

And yes, people do click on the links in your footer.

My homepage is quite long. Yet, people scroll till the end, click to read my articles, watch my video and even follow me on social by clicking the links in the footer.

How many visitors are leaving your website too soon because you have an empty footer?

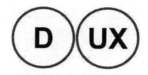

#24: Don't make your text lines as wide as the whole desktop screen

You spend hours writing your posts, but if your visitors can't read them with ease you've wasted your efforts: They'll get tired after a couple of paragraphs and just leave.

One of the things that make reading hard is having too wide text lines.

What's the best line width for web content?

It's not necessarily 50-75 characters per line as you may have heard. The studies that suggest this:

- Were done on printed medium and not web pages
- Didn't segment people surveyed by age (how do you know if they were the same age as your target audience?)
- Didn't specify which font type and size were used

What is the best line width then?

It's the line width that doesn't require a noticeable extra effort from your visitors to read your text.

Meaning:

- They don't have to turn their heads left and right to follow the lines (lines are too long).
- They don't have to move their eye pupils too fast (lines are too short).

The rule of thumb: Assuming your monitor is wider than it's tall, the text line should occupy about 50% of the desktop screen width. The remaining 50% should be white space. This means:

- either use equal left and right margins (25% of the screen width each)

- or use less white space on the left but more white space on the right.

If you aren't sure whether the length of the text lines on your website is fine, ask a couple of friends to read the text on your pages and see if they find it difficult.

Don't make the text lines stretch all the way from left to right

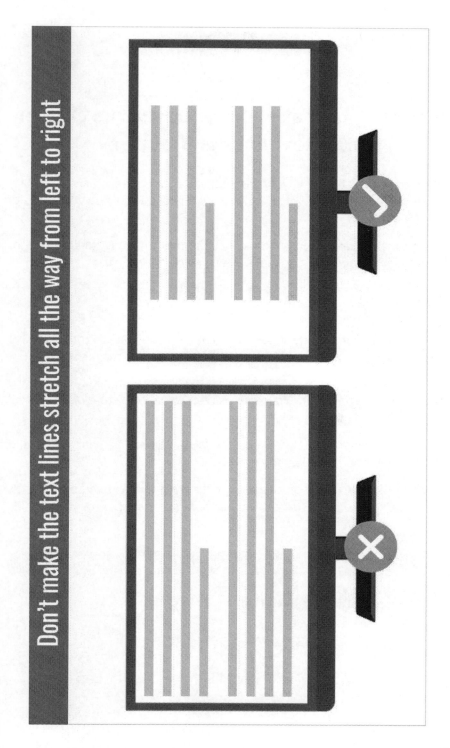

#25: How to make sure your visitors click on your text links and buttons

When someone is browsing your website, you aren't there in person to point somewhere and shout, *"Hey, click here!"*. You have to rely on your website to do that for you.

So, if you want people to click on something, make sure it stands out from the rest of the page and also looks like something clickable.

To make sure your visitors click on your links:

- Make the links stand out from the rest of the text
- Make your important call-to-action links look like buttons and give them a color that stands out from your theme's main colors

If you want your visitors to click on a link to visit another page, don't make the link look like an image. Your visitors don't expect a picture placed within some text to be a link and won't click on it.

Make the visual distinction between text and clickable elements (links and buttons) crystal clear.

For example, your headings should look like plain text and not like buttons. Otherwise, you add to visual clutter and confuse your visitors.

Make sure your text links stand out

✔ Here's a **link** that stands out

✔ This **link** will also get noticed

✘ This link will most likely be overlooked

#26: Avoid saying this on your website so you don't come across as condescending

Isn't running a website fun? There are infinite ways you can mess it up!

So, it makes sense to talk about at least two such ways in this chapter – two phrases that make you sound condescending.

1) Research suggests that...

... as in "Research suggests that 80% of new businesses fail."

What are you trying to do here? Scare your prospects into hiring you?

"Will I be among those 80%? Oh no! Let's hire this person who knows the cool stats!"

This won't work. "Research suggests" is unspecific (What research? In what niche? Among businesses of what size?) and, thus, feels irrelevant to your prospects.

Yes, citing research can boost your authority and credibility. But only if it features your target audience and their specific problems, not when it's some generic study.

2) If you're a business owner...

... as in "If you're a business owner, you know that copy helps you sell more."

But if you know I know, why are you telling me this? And if I don't know, should I feel bad about it?

Plus, if your target audience *is* business owners, what's the point of doing the "if" dance?

With a sentence like that, you can only lose.

I get it. You're trying to show that you understand your prospects. But there are better ways to do it.

Be clear about what you want each sentence to achieve and say it directly:

- Want to point out a fear they may feel? Say, *"Are you afraid of X?"*

- Want to point out a benefit of your offer? Don't imply your prospects know it. Tell them why it's the case and how it will make their lives easier.

#27: How to make sure your web page will resonate with your prospects

When writing content for your website, it's easy to get lost in detail.

Is this the right word to use? How does this font look? Where should I put this image?

But although these things are important, you need to make sure you get the basics right first.

Here are the seven must-have features of a compelling page that works.

1) Relevant:

Make sure your content:

- Is relevant to your audience
- Matches their expectations
- Delivers on the promise of the title

2) Clear:

- Make sure your copy is clear, not clever.
- Don't use meaningless words or jargon.
- Make important information or elements visually prominent.
- Make logically related elements visually related.

3) Valuable:

- Put your readers' needs first.
- Offer solutions and actionable tips.

4) Trustworthy:

- Use correct grammar and spelling.

- Don't use superlatives, ?!?! or WORDS IN ALL CAPS.
- Support all your claims with proof.

5) Minimum distractions:

- Don't autoplay audio or video.
- Think twice before using carousels or pop-ups.
- Don't use excessive animations or ads.

6) Minimum friction:

- Make everything on your page easy to read and use.

7) Actionable:

- Create every page with one action in mind (except your homepage, see Chapter #19, page 34).
- Make your CTAs prominent and use compelling copy.

#28: Treat your website navigation as a part of your business message

Compare these two examples.

Navigation A:

HOME | ABOUT | SERVICES | BLOG | CONTACT

Navigation B:

HOME | ABOUT | COURSES | BOOKS | BLOG | CONTACT

Who just told you more about their business?

Person A could be anybody. But person B is in the coaching business ("Courses") and has probably been doing it for a while ("Books").

Whether these courses and books are any good is a different story. But for now, smart person B gets brownie points.

To make your navigation support your business message:

- Use clear and succinct navigation labels
- Include specific navigation labels that give your prospects an idea of what you do

Examples:

- "Demo" communicates that you're a SaaS company
- "Courses" shows that you're in the coaching business
- "Website review" indicates that you review websites

Main navigation Don'ts:

- Linking to less important pages (for example, "Impressum", "Privacy policy")
- Not linking to important pages (for example, "About us", "Services")

- Placing navigation labels in unexpected places – anywhere else than at the top of the page (on the side, at the bottom, or having orphaned navigation labels in the left corner because your main navigation breaks in two rows, etc.)

#29: Three things that will ruin the most beautiful and eloquent website

Websites are like houses. If you build them on sand, it doesn't matter how pretty they are, because they won't be standing there for long.

Here are three things that can ruin even the best-looking and the best-sounding website:

- You don't know your services / products well enough.
- Your target audience is 'everybody'.
- You haven't decided on your website's purpose.

So, before writing a single line for your website, make sure that you:

1) **Get clear about your product or services**

- What does your product do exactly? / What services do you offer?
- What are its benefits / what problems does it solve?

2) **Zero in on your target audience**

- What kind of people are most likely to love your product or services? The most beautiful website will fail to grow your business if it's targeting the wrong audience.

3) **Define the purpose of your website**

- How will your website help your business? For example, get new clients, sell your product, promote your brand, earn money with affiliate marketing, etc.
- What pages do you need to reach that goal? Make a list.
- Do you need a blog? If yes, what will be your blog's focus and how will it contribute to the main purpose of your website?
- Are you going to grow your email list? If yes, how?

#30: An ultra-practical way to come up with a great headline when you're struggling to be creative

Have you heard of creative limitation? It's an idea that setting restrictions on your final result will force you to be more creative and to try harder.

Here's how you can apply this principle to create a great headline or email subject line every time.

Step #1:

Write what your post / newsletter is about using as many words as you need to get clarity for yourself and discover specific words you may want to use later.

Step #2:

Come up with at least one headline for each of these formulas[*]:

- How I've achieved a major goal
- Super-curiosity
- Do it like this famous person
- Learn something without pain
- The super-valuable resource
- Stop struggling
- What nobody gets (but is super-important)

See the image at the end of this chapter for examples.

Step #3:

For each headline, calculate its CoSchedule[**] and Advanced Marketing Institute[***] headline score, and their average.

Step #4:

Combine the scores your headlines received with your knowledge about your audience to select the winner.

* – I got the idea for these formulas from an article by Henneke Duistermaat called "7 Steal-Worthy Emails to Boost Clicks (and Blog Readers)".

** – Use free online Headline Analyzer tool from CoSchedule.

*** – Use free online Emotional Marketing Value Headline Analyzer tool from Advanced Marketing Institute.

Formula	Headline
How I've achieved a major goal	Struggling to come up with engaging headlines? Follow these 9 steps to get it done in no time
Super-curiosity	Did you know that you can create a perfect headline just by filling in an Excel spreadsheet?
Do it like this famous person	Creating engaging headlines: A step-by-step process stolen from a famous copywriter
Learn something without pain	How to come up with a perfect headline without actually trying
The super-valuable resource	Fill in this Excel spreadsheet to create a headline your readers can't ignore
Stop struggling	How to come up with better headlines in less time
What nobody gets (but is super-important)	Writing engaging headlines: Set boundaries for your creativity to come up with a better headline in less time

#31: How to use (and not to use) your photographs on your website

Do you know what helps you instantly connect with your website visitors?

Your face!

Your photograph on your website helps your visitors know, like and trust you faster than 100 words. But only if you do it the right way.

Here are some dos and don'ts of using your photographs on a business website.

Don'ts:

- Low resolution
- Busy background
- Shadows on the face
- Looking away from the text on the page
- Other people or animals in the photograph
- Face taking up too little space of the photograph (for example, if you're standing too far away from the camera)

Dos:

- High resolution photograph
- Plain background
- Face taking up the most space in the photograph
- Friendly facial expression
- Facing straight at or towards the text and / or call-to-action button

Do you have your photograph or the headshots of your team members on your homepage? If not, use this easy way to make your visitors know, like and trust you faster.

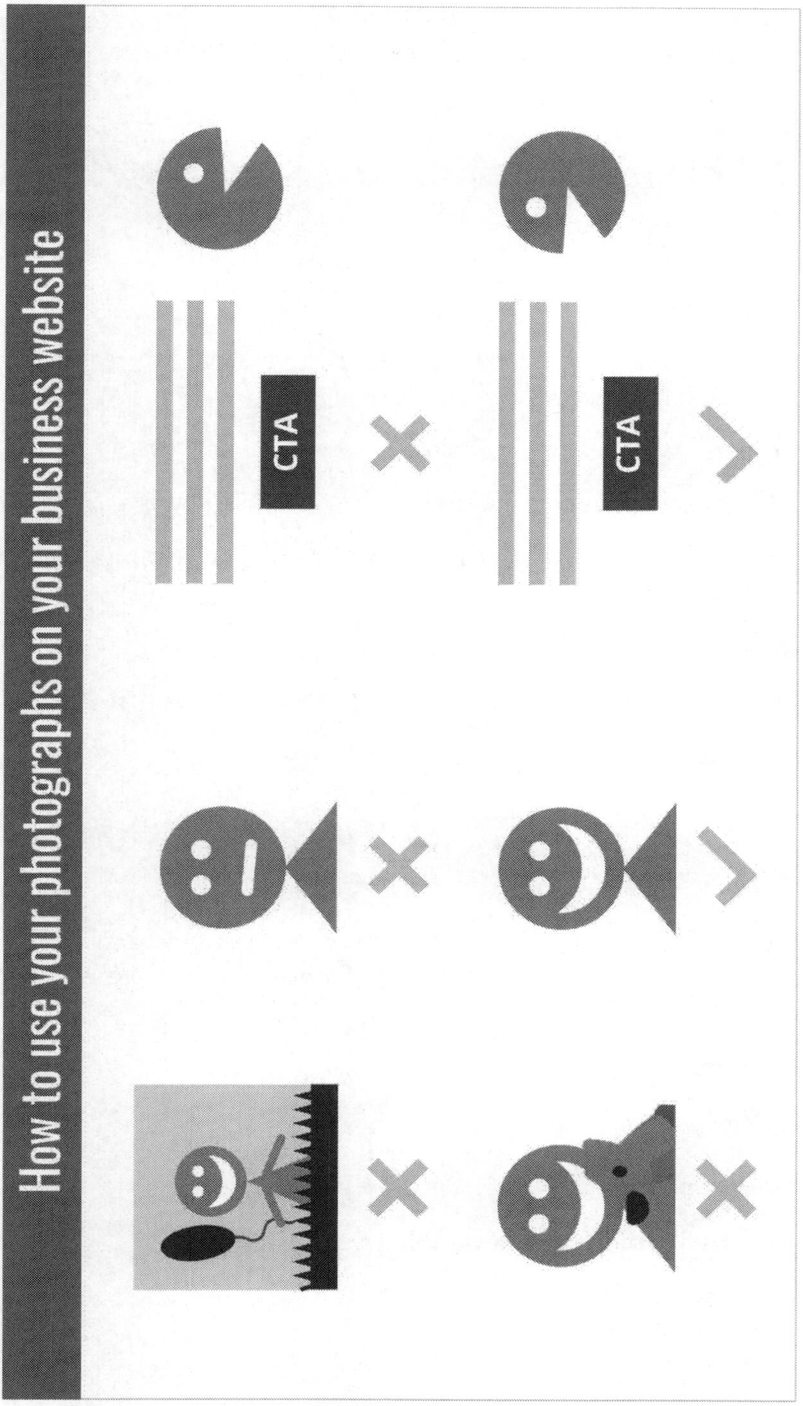
How to use your photographs on your business website
CTA
CTA

#32: This one emotion kills your conversions

(Ha, I think it rhymes!)

This emotion is fear.

Fear that you won't do a good job. Fear that your product won't fit their needs. Fear that they won't like you, etc.

This results in a feeling of uncertainty.

And when your visitors feel uncertain, they won't hire you or buy from you.

Here are five reasons why your prospects may feel uncertain (and what to do about it).

1) Not sure what you mean

"I'm not sure what she offers. I don't understand this sentence."

Always be crystal clear in your copy.

2) Not sure about your fees

"What are her fees? Is it per hour / project / day?"

State your fees openly, mention a range or tell your prospects what your fees depend on to help them understand if your services are within their budget.

3) Not sure how it works

"What happens after I contact her?"

Explain your process.

4) Not sure if you'll do a good job

"Is she any good? What if I'm not happy?"

Use client testimonials. State what happens if your client is unsatisfied with the results or the product.

5) Not sure if you'll get along

"Will I like her?"

Include your photograph (even better, a video) and let your personality shine through.

#33: How to improve readability of your content (and keep visitors on your website longer)

When your visitors land on your website, they don't start reading immediately.

First, they'll skim your page. And only when they find something that seems relevant, they'll dive into it.

Help them find what they're looking for faster, keep their attention when they start reading, and they'll stay longer and read more.

How to improve readability of your content:

- Use a minimum font size of 16px for body text. If your target audience is older, consider using a larger font size.

- Make your paragraphs short (maximum four to five lines).

- Don't overdo it with one-liners either. Five one-sentence paragraphs after another are also hard to skim.

- Use headings and subheadings while paying attention to visual hierarchy.

- Use different styling for subheadings of the different levels. If both section and subsection headings have the same style, your visitors will have to spend extra effort to understand the structure of the page.

- Use bullet points, italic or bold highlights or block quotes.

- Don't overdo it with the highlights though. If every third word of your paragraph is bold, it'll have the opposite effect.

- Use images to break visual monotony.

#34: Want more prospects to convert? Build a bridge

Why is good copy important?

You may be tempted to answer, *"Because it helps sell your product (duh!)"*.

And you would be right. But this short explanation doesn't really show *how* important it is.

I was asked on a podcast once why copy is important, and I remembered a game I used to play as a kid.

You had to build a bridge between two points and then run a simulation letting a train cross it. Once the train starts moving, you can't intervene.

If your bridge doesn't collapse, the train reaches the other side. You get bonus points and go to another level.

But if you have no idea how to make a strong bridge and are just guessing where to put your building blocks, the train won't make it over (trust me, the 14-year-old me tried to wing it but couldn't get past level 2).

Your copy is a lot like that.

It's a bridge between the place your prospects are in now and the place where they need to be to convert.

You can't build your bridge in a hurry. Nor let it be built by someone who isn't an engineer.

Because a good bridge isn't just a collection of bricks. The same way as good copy isn't just a collection of words.

#35: You don't need an FAQ page. Here's what you need instead

Do you really need an FAQ page? Sometimes you do, but most often you don't. Here are some pros and cons for FAQ pages.

Pros:

- Saves you time
- Weeds out bad leads
- Reassures your ideal clients that you're what they need
- Can boost your SEO

Cons:

- Not many people will visit it
- When someone has a question on another page, they may not think of checking your FAQ page and leave your website instead, because they haven't got their question answered

What to add to your website instead of an FAQ page?

Instead of lumping all the questions about all of your offers on one page, anticipate the questions your prospects may have on every page and provide the answers on the spot:

- On your homepage
- On your Contact page
- On service / product pages
- On the Checkout page

This is especially important when you ask your prospects to take an action but anticipate particular reservations.

If you do decide to have an FAQ page:

- Structure it for easy navigation

- Make it scannable

- List the most often-asked questions first

- Make the answers succinct and to the point

- Don't duplicate existing content; instead, link to the in-depth pages, if necessary

- Link to your Contact page at the end, encouraging people to contact you if they haven't found the answer to their question

#36: Make the copy of your CTA buttons boring

Don't try to be creative with the copy on your call-to-action buttons. Instead, make sure it's crystal clear and (ideally) works out of context.

Here's how.

Use an imperative.

The CTA button copy should complete the phrase "I'd like you to...", as in "[I'd like you to...] Download your ebook".

"Download my ebook" is also fine. But if your CTA says "Info" or "More", it's a bad CTA. Because nobody would like 'to info', and no one would like 'to more'.

If possible, make your CTA copy work out of context.

Use "Learn more" as a CTA only if it's clear to your website visitors what they'll be learning more about. Otherwise, you may create unnecessary friction by forcing your visitors to spend more time figuring out what this button does than is necessary.

In every case, make your CTA copy clear, because people older than five won't click on a button unless they know exactly where it leads.

Make your CTA copy clear and actionable

Find out more

Book a free consultation

Download my ebook

View services

Register for this webinar

More info

Become a hero

Evolve with it

Why case studies

Shut up and take my money

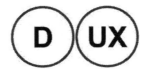

#37: One design mistake that ruins all your bullet points

"Use bullet points in your copy. It improves readability."

Great advice that completely forgets to warn you about one crucial mistake.

Many websites use numbered lists or bullet points without separating individual items with white space, which turns those lists into walls of text with black circles or numbers sprinkled on the side.

And guess what? Nobody likes to read through a wall of text, even if it comes with decorations.

The solution to this problem is to add some CSS code to your website theme. Sounds scary, I know. But I have something you can copy-paste.

Here's what you need do.

Open your custom CSS file. Scroll to the very bottom and copy-paste these two lines:

```
article ul li, article ol li {margin-top: 24px}

article ul > : last-child, article ol > : last-child
{margin-bottom: 24px}
```

In human speak, it means:

"For both bullet points and numbered lists, add 24px of white space before every point. Also, make sure the last point has 24px of distance from the next paragraph."

You can tweak "24px" to suit your theme.

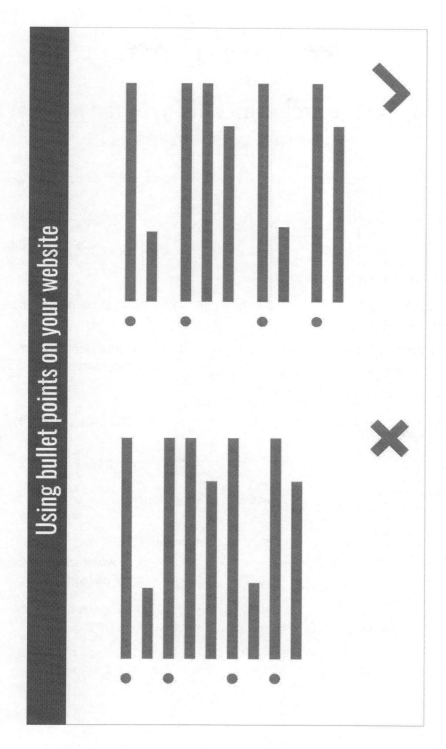

Using bullet points on your website

#38: How to create an effective lead magnet (and grow your list faster)

No, lead magnets aren't dead. And whoever spreads this rumor is simply doing it wrong.

But first, a quick question: What do you need a lead magnet for?

If you answered "to get more subscribers", you aren't seeing the big picture.

You need a lead magnet to:

... get more subscribers who are genuinely interested in what you have to say,

... who will amplify your message

... and either become your customers themselves

... or bring their friends who will buy from you.

For a lead magnet to accomplish that, it must be:

- **Targeted** so that your new subscribers will also be interested in your email newsletter, other content and paid offers
- **Ultra-helpful** to demonstrate your expertise in solving your audience's problems
- **Actionable** to make sure they implement it and see real results from your free advice
- **Easy to consume** so that your audience doesn't feel overwhelmed
- **Impressive** to make sure your new subscribers remember you and will recognize your name next time it pops up in their inbox

Bonus tip: If you can create a dedicated page for your lead magnet and make it rank in search, you'll get a constant flow of subscribers without lifting a finger.

#39: How to tell if you should implement that new website tip you just read about

All great websites are great in the same way. They:

- Are structured with clear goals in mind
- Have visual hierarchy that makes sense
- Are easy to skim and read
- Have relevant content written in the language of their audience
- Have minimum distractions and offer as little friction in user experience as possible

But every bad website is bad in its own way, because "goals", "distraction", "visual hierarchy that makes sense", etc. have specific and often different meanings for every website.

Want to know if you should implement that website tip you just read about?

Ask yourself:

"If I implement this, will it help my visitors do something I want them to do on this page?"

(read an article with a lead magnet, check out your books, check out Services page, etc.)

"... or will it steer them in the wrong direction?"

(drive their attention to an unimportant element, take them to another website, annoy them, etc.)

You can't blindly trust any tip you read about, even if it's coming from a recognized expert. But such tips are examples of a certain meta idea, which is usually useful.

Isolate that idea and decide if this tip is the best way to implement it on your website.

Here's an example.

Tip: "Use opt-in pop-ups on your website to grow your list."

Meta idea: "To grow your list, display your sign-up form in a prominent way."

To decide if you should implement this tip on your website, consider if using a pop-up would be the best way to make your sign-up form visually prominent or if you could think of another way to do that on your website that better fits your business model.

#40: Don't interfere with the natural reading patterns of your visitors

Can your visitors follow the flow of your content with ease? Consider the three examples given below of arranging your content on a page.

One column

A no-brainer. Your visitors will read from top to bottom.

One wide column + one narrow column

That's a no-brainer as well. They know that the main text is in the wide column and that the narrow column is a sidebar.

Yet, studies show that website visitors don't pay much attention to the content in sidebars. Plus, if it has visually prominent elements, it may distract them from the main content.

So, although your visitors will know how to read your page, they may not do it in the way you wanted them to.

Two equal columns

Now your visitors are struggling. Obviously, you want them to read the left column from top to bottom and then the right column from top to bottom. But they can't concentrate, as it's not a natural reading pattern.

Plus, the visual highlights in both columns are pulling their attention in different directions.

Here's how to guide your visitors and make sure they read your page in the order you want them to with ease:

- Structure your page based on a natural reading pattern:
  - F: Reading the first couple of lines in full and then scrolling down, skimming the left side

- o Z: Reading the first lines in full, then skimming diagonally before reading the bottom lines
- To make them follow a different path, use clear visual hierarchy placing the highlights along that path (and nowhere else).

Don't interfere with the common reading patterns

#41: How to use (and not to use) questions in your copy

Using questions in your copy is tricky, because you can accidentally mislead your prospects or provoke an undesired reaction.

Two things to keep in mind to make questions in your copy work in your favor.

#1 Use only questions that get you a "yes"

If your question prompts a "no" or "I don't know" reaction, you have a problem.

Ready to upgrade your plan?

(Who's ever ready to upgrade?)

Would you like to work together?

(Not sure yet.)

Do you need magic content?

(What will it do for me?)

Especially in your website headline or on a sales page, it's important that the questions you ask get you a 100% "yes".

The best way to ensure that is to communicate the benefit in the question. For example:

Want to do more in less time?

(Sure!)

Want to grow your business faster?

(Who doesn't?)

Want to sell more?

(Yes!)

In case you aren't sure if your question will get you a "yes" from your target audience, play it safe and go with a declarative sentence.

To clarify: You only need a "yes" from your target audience, not 100% of your website visitors. If someone who's not a good fit would answer the questions in your copy with a "no", that's fine.

#2 Don't use too many questions

Are you struggling with this? Do you feel like this? Maybe you feel like this? What if you could feel like this? Or like this? Or fix this problem?

#ohcomeon

Every time you pose a question, it creates friction.

Think of these questions as speed bumps: Your visitors will be fine if you shake them a couple of times, but nobody appreciates miles of a bumpy road.

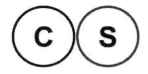

#42: How to feature your services on your homepage to get more client inquiries

How do you feature your services on your homepage?

As a long piece of text that your prospects have no chance of understanding quickly?

Or as an ocean of icons, text snippets and buttons that overload your prospects with options?

Here's a better solution. Feature your services as a few succinct sections and call-to-action buttons that your prospects can't help but click.

Have two to four sections with the following structure:

Service name: Curb your creativity and use the words your prospects would use to describe this service.

- Not like this: "Marketing Mastery"
- But like this: "Marketing on Social Media"

Two to three sentences that highlight the problems this service solves and how it helps solve them.

CTA button: Nothing creative. Ideally, something specific like "View packages", "Get a quote", etc. When in doubt, go with "Learn more".

Use the icons wisely and make sure they don't steal the show from the CTA buttons. Not sure how to do that? Ditch the icons altogether.

Pro tip: Have more than four services? Group some of them together on your homepage in categories and split them into separate sections later, on the page your prospects will land after clicking the corresponding CTA.

How to feature your services on your homepage

SERVICES

I do this that helps people like that solve these problems

SERVICE 1

Do you have this problem?
Are you struggling with
this? I can do this for you
and this is how it helps
solve your problems.

LEARN MORE

SERVICE 2

Do you have this problem?
Are you struggling with
this? I can do this for you
and this is how it helps
solve your problems.

VIEW PACKAGES

SERVICE 3

Do you have this problem?
Are you struggling with this?
I can do this for you and
this is how it helps solve
your problems.

LEARN MORE

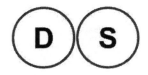

#43: How to create a newsletter opt-in that actually gets you subscribers

Do you know what makes your visitors sign up for your newsletter?

Not your opt-in. Your content!

If your content is boring, nobody will sign up for your newsletter, no matter where you put your opt-in and what words or colors you use.

Here's how to create an opt-in that gets you subscribers.

Heading: Make it clear and visually prominent so that it signals to those who were impressed with your post that there's an option to get your precious tips delivered straight into their inbox.

Text: Make it short. State the benefits and set expectations. If you already have an impressive list, use social proof. For example, "Join 5000 of your peers".

Button: Use copy that works out of context:

- Not like this: "Yes, please!"
- But like this: "Sign up"

Pro tip: No need to say, "I won't spam you". If your site looks credible, the thought of spam won't even cross your readers' mind (and you shouldn't put it there).

Believe it or not, if you publish good stuff, your website visitors will want to sign up for your newsletter. You just need to clearly show them the way and give them a gentle nudge in the right direction.

Effective newsletter opt-in

Follow this blog by entering your email here:

Sign up for my newsletter "The Magic of Words", and I'll send you the most relevant tips and "how to" guides.

YES, PLEASE!

No spam. Promised.

Want more client inquiries?

Get my best tips delivered directly into your inbox every Thursday.

SIGN UP

#44: Three ways to identify your target audience

If you feel like next time someone tells you to identify your target audience you're going to slap them in the face, I hear you.

This advice gets repeated often. Yet, the recommended method often sounds too abstract.

Here are three concrete ways to identify your target audience.

1) The Imaginary

Turn your imagination on... and fill out a questionnaire*.

No clients yet? Try to imagine those who need your product / service most. How old are they? Where do they work? What do they worry about?

2) The Easy

Think about your favorite clients and what they have in common... and fill out a questionnaire*.

3) The Lucky

Think about yourself... and fill out a questionnaire*.

This one goes against the popular advice, which is "you're not your customer".

But chances are, even if you aren't now, you were once struggling with the same problems as you now claim to solve. And if you can remember those times, you can identify your target audience.

* – There is no way around it. The best way to get clarity on your ideal clients is to put their traits on paper. Need a questionnaire? Download one here: **gillandrews.com/ideal-client-profile**.

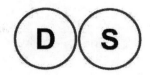

#45: Include a call to action on every page of your website (and even in your freebies)

You know the saying "Strike while the iron's hot"? The hot iron in question is your engaged visitor.

She has read your page, and she is excited. Now it's time to strike – by giving her an opportunity to take your relationship further and presenting her with a call to action.

Here are some actions you can ask your visitors to take on your pages or even your lead magnet PDFs.

Homepage (multiple CTAs):

Contact / View services / View a post with a freebie / Sign up for updates

About page (single CTA):

Contact / Sign up for updates

Services page (single CTA):

Contact / Fill out a form / Book an appointment

Blog post (multiple CTA):

Download a resource / Sign up for updates

Resource PDF (multiple CTA):

Check out your homepage / Check out another ultra-useful post

"Thank you" page (single CTA):

Follow you on social / Take a survey

FAQ page:

Contact you (if they haven't found the answer) / Check out additional resources on your website

Don't rely on your visitors to come back to the navigation and select another page. Offer them a logical next step on the spot. Because with every additional page they read they get to know, like and trust you more.

#46: Five reasons why using a one-page website is a bad idea

You must have seen it: It looks like a usual website, but its navigation labels don't open any new pages. Instead, they take you to a different section on the same page.

One-page websites.

You may be tempted to get one because you want to keep it simple. Plus, you don't have much info to share. So, the fewer the pages, the less the trouble, right?

Nope.

Here are five reasons you don't want a one-pager:

1) You're confusing your visitors

You know it's a one-pager. For your visitors, it looks like a 'normal' website (because... navigation). So, they expect it to behave like one.

They click on the "Services" navigation label and start reading, but the page doesn't end with the Services info. It continues with your About section or whatever you put next.

This may be relevant info per se but causes confusion here as it contradicts their expectations.

2) You're putting constraints on your copy

OK, you don't have much to say now. But what if you want to add a new service or start blogging? Are you ready to go through some major website changes in a year?

3) Your page takes longer to load

Your one-page website is first of all a page – one URL for all the content. And this content will take longer to load than if you split it between multiple URLs (i.e. different pages on your website).

Especially if your one-pager has a lot of visuals, you'll be asking your visitors to wait longer for the page to load, and not everyone will do that.

4) It's bad for SEO

It's about 1,000,000 times more difficult to rank with one page than with many, especially in a saturated niche.

5) You won't get any insights on user behavior

Google Analytics doesn't record which navigation labels get clicked if they don't lead to a separate page. So, you won't have any data to see what works and what doesn't.

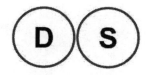

#47: Remove links from your homepage, About and sales pages

You know how I can tell if a website owner is also a frequent blogger? They treat their homepage, About and sales pages like blog posts and just looove using text links in the body copy.

But, while linking to a related article in a blog post is a good idea because it may help your visitors find more / better answers to their questions,

... it's an absolute conversion killer on your homepage, About and sales pages.

Why?

Because those pages have a different goal: not to just let your visitors wander aimlessly around your website but to deliver a mini presentation persuading them to take one specific action (contact you, download a freebie, etc.).

Think about it. If you were giving a presentation in real life, would you open a door and ask your audience if they'd like to leave in the middle of it?

Of course not! But that's exactly what happens if you have a text link in the middle of a sentence on pages that talk about what you do and for whom or describe your products or services.

Have important info you'd like your prospects to learn while they're reading your page? Don't give them a link to a different page but communicate that info in plain text right there.

The only elements with a link on your homepage, About or sales pages should be prominent calls to action (the fewer, the better). This gives you more control over how your prospects read your copy and increases the chances of them clicking that CTA button.

Remove in-text links from your sales pages

About

▬▬ my blog post

● ● ● ●

▬▬ company I worked for
▬▬ my other website

▬▬ Contact me

✕

About

● ● ● ●

Want to find out what's holding you back?

GET IN TOUCH

>

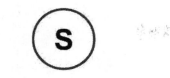

#48: How to lure more prospects to your website from search

Has this ever happened to you?

You went to see an apartment for rent. You arrive at the address and see a shabby building with a filthy door. You turn around and leave immediately without even going in.

That's how your prospects feel when they see your 'shabby' meta titles and meta descriptions in search results.

Your website is your house, and what your prospects see about it in search is the entrance door. If you want them to come in, that door needs to be pretty.

Here's how to lure more prospects to your website from search.

A **meta title** should have at least one of these characteristics (ideally, several):

- Ultra-specific
- Useful
- Urgent
- Unique

A **meta description** should:

- Use "you" more than "I" / "we"
- Address a problem your prospects are facing
- Promise a benefit
- Appeal to their current emotional state

To make sure Google doesn't cut your titles and descriptions before you've made your point, stick to these character limits:

- Meta title: 50-60 characters
- Meta description: 50-160 characters

Want more visitors to your website? Treat meta titles and meta descriptions the same way you treat your sales copy.

Pay attention to how your prospects see you in search

The Writingale - Home
https://writingale.com/ ▼
The Writingale. Select page. Home - About - Services - Work with me - Contact

The Writingale - Free Copywriting Course
https://writingale.com/free-course/ ▼
Free copywriting course. Is your website not getting you enough clients, leads or business? Not sure which techniques...

The Writingale - Home
https://writingale.com/ ▼
Web writing tips and copywriting courses for busy creatives.

Free Copywriting Course for Beginners
https://writingale.com/free-course/ ▼
Learn how to write irresistible web copy to attract ideal clients and grow your business.

#49: Make your prospects trust you more by being specific

Imagine your son comes home later than usual. You ask him where he's been. Which answer would sound more believable?

a) I got held up at school.

b) Mr. Johnson asked me to stay after class to discuss that play we're performing on Friday, and I missed my bus.

It's b), isn't it? Because it's more specific.

If your son gives you a vague answer, you can still ask additional questions. But as your visitors can't do that, you have only one shot to make your copy sound believable on your website.

Here's how to use specificity to make the claims on your website more believable.

In your value proposition:

Copy that sells => Personality-driven copy for creative businesses

In product descriptions:

Fresh strawberries => Strawberries picked this morning

In blog post titles:

Ultimate website checklist => Ultimate website checklist 2019

In a freebie title:

Comprehensive ebook => 42-page ebook

In a newsletter opt-in:

Join your peers => Join 5,000+ peers

In social proof:

Mike did a great job => Our conversion rate went up 24%

We have great reviews => We have 1,426 5-star reviews

#50: When you should ditch storytelling and get straight to the point

There's this hyped-up technique doing the rounds these days called "storytelling". I'm sure you've heard of it, but in the unlikely case you haven't...

Storytelling in marketing means that instead of using a lot of data and complicated business-like words, you're supposed to tell a story. A story of a hero who struggles in life but then discovers your product and suddenly solves all his problems.

But guess what? Everyone else with blogs and things to sell heard of it, too. And now wherever you look: long stories and lots of telling.

Yet, storytelling isn't a silver bullet, because sometimes the best story you can tell goes like this:

"Hi, want this checklist, like on this picture but with bigger letters and checkboxes? Then click this button."

(The end)

This straight-shooter approach works well when you know that people who land on your page don't want to hear the 'why' and are ready to hear the 'what'.

The image at the end of this chapter illustrates a test I ran for one of my lead magnets.

Its original version had lots of storytelling before the lead magnet was even visible. The moment I cut the 'whys' and made that infographic visible above the fold, the conversion rate shot up.

You can try this approach on the following pages on your website:

- Informational pages that answer a question "What is...?"

- Freebies

- Pages that target prospects who are already aware of your offer and the problems it solves (aka "solution-aware")

Ditch storytelling and get to the point fast

Website Checklist 2019

(short description)

Link to download

(One ultra-long infographic)

Grab this checklist as a handy PDF
Why PDF is better than this article

Download

(listing points in detail)

Above the fold

Website Checklist 2019

(trying to be funny)

(telling a story of how you created this list)

(link to another page)

(One ultra-long infographic)

Download this checklist as PDF

Download

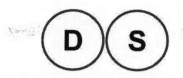

#51: Want people to stay on your page longer? Treat headings like a table of contents

Most of your website visitors won't read your page like a book, attentively from top to bottom. They'll start by scrolling down, scanning the headings, looking for a section that seems most relevant.

Suddenly, your page headings become a table of contents your visitors check to see what 'chapter' they want to read, and they will only start reading when they see a 'chapter title' that seems relevant.

Can you guess what happens if your 'table of contents' is vague, and your visitors don't understand what each section is about?

Right, they leave.

To make your visitors stay on your page longer:

- Use unambiguous titles to clearly communicate what each section is about:
  - Not like this: Here's the key / What does this mean? / Why?
  - But like this: My services / About / Happy clients
- Use typical phrasing to reduce the time and effort it takes to process the info:
  - Not like this: A writer turned copywriter / Here's what I can do for you
  - But like this: About me / Services / Get in touch

Here's a fun exercise: Open your homepage and check out the section headings. What do they say?

Treat page headings like a table of contents

Rachel Green, Technical Copywriter

Here's the key

Who am I?

What does it mean?

Let's go!

Rachel Green, Technical Copywriter

Services

About Rachel

Happy clients

Get in touch!

#52: Use social proof that's meaningful to your prospects (and not just your ego)

Raise your hand if you tell your prospects all about your education and career path or display badges on your website (you know, the organizations you're a member of or certificates that you have).

Now, think about what you do when you're looking for a new doctor.

Do you check what school they went to and what training they completed? Or do you read the reviews of their patients?

Exactly! All that name-dropping and badge-flashing pales in significance in front of the real client testimonials because your prospects:

- Don't care what university you went to

- May have never heard of the companies you worked for

- May have never heard of the organization you belong to (or, worse, have heard of it but know that anyone who pays a fee can become a member)

What your prospects do care about is what real people like them who have worked with you say about your offers.

So, make sure you use social proof that's meaningful to your prospects (and not only to your ego).

Exception: Name-dropping does help if you worked for a famous company. Don't link out to their website though. Just mention their name and say what results you've achieved for them.

Use social proof meaningful to your customers (not your ego)

About

uni I studied at

my other website

organization I'm a member of

A
B
C

XYZ

PROCOPYWRITERS
member

About

uni I studied at

a fun fact that makes me relatable

how I can help

"Great result achieved"

(testimonial)

CONTACT ME

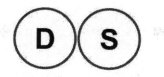

#53: How to make sure your contact forms are easy to spot and use

Sure, if someone is heavily impressed by you, they'll find a way to contact you.

But what if they're still on the fence? Or have multiple tabs open and are comparing you to your competitors?

Then a contact form that's difficult to spot and / or use can cost you a valuable inquiry.

Here's how to make your contact forms visible and accessible.

1) Make your form look like a form:

- Placeholder text should look different from the body text (for example, gray italic).

- Input fields should look like input fields – white boxes with a thin border.

- "Submit" button should be visually prominent and look like a button.

2) Ask only for absolutely necessary data

If your form has multiple fields, visitors perceive the task of filling it out as complicated and time-consuming. Plus, not everyone is comfortable with sharing their phone number. So, only ask for it if it's really necessary.

Anticipating some reservations? Add a line explaining why you need that particular information.

Pro tip #1: Have a page selling a service? Include a contact form right there so that your visitors can complete it on the spot.

Pro tip #2: Get rid of "Subject" input field on your page by setting it to something fixed in your form settings (for example, "New inquiry"). If using multiple in-page forms, give them different subjects based on the page (for example, "New inquiry: Website copy").

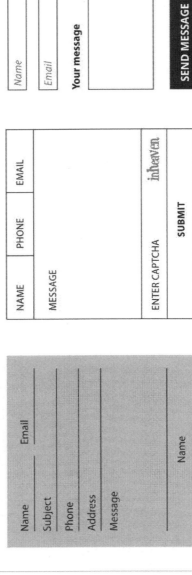

Make your contact form easy to spot and use

Name

Email

Your message

SEND MESSAGE

NAME	PHONE	EMAIL
MESSAGE		

ENTER CAPTCHA inheaven

SUBMIT

Name

Subject

Phone

Address

Message

Email

Name

#54: Use this test to quickly spot vague copy that will confuse your prospects

Have you ever landed on a website and not been able to figure out what they offer?

Surprisingly, you're very good at spotting vague copy on the websites of others, but your BS detector seems to malfunction when it comes to your own website.

Here's a quick trick to spot vague copy on your website (aka "The BS test").

Imagine using the same words you use on your web page in a real conversation while talking to a prospect.

Will she understand you right away? Or will you need to explain further?

– *So, what do you do, Jane?*

– *We execute engaging brand experiences.*

#awkwardsilence

Oops, your copy is vague. What now?

- Rewrite it using clear plain words. Use as many words as necessary to get your point across but not a word more.

- If it's a complicated concept, use a real-world analogy.

- If it's your website tagline, use one of these formulas:

{What} for {whom}

Branding and design for creative women entrepreneurs

{Do this} to / and {get the benefit}

Turn your underperforming website into a lead-generating machine

{What} {with what benefit}

Web copy that wins your prospects' hearts (and wallets)

{Get this benefit} {by doing this}

Turn lurkers into loyal customers with personality-driven copy

Helping {whom} {do what} {with what benefit}

Helping marketers publish research that gets attention

Done? Now reapply the BS test and see if you passed this time.

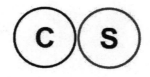

#55: Separate the benefits you describe on a page by context

Mention the benefits of your offer, they said. Your visitors will like it, they said.

What can possibly go wrong?

Here's another question.

How does it help a prospect who wants to hire you to write a blog post to read about how your copy makes products irresistible?

Yet, that's exactly what happens when you lump together the benefits of multiple products or offers.

Sure, it matters that your prospects learn about the benefits of your offers. But it also matters *where* and *when* they learn about them.

You should mention the benefits of your copy when describing your copywriting services. And the benefits of your blogging skills in the blogging services section, etc.

This way you make sure that:

- Every visitor gets the information relevant to their goals
- Important parts get the attention they deserve, as there are now fewer sentences on the page competing for the reader's attention

So, mention the benefits where they matter and when they matter (and not anywhere and at a random time).

You'll find an example on the next page. Notice how the last point on the left side doesn't fit the rest (blog posts aren't supposed to sell your product; web copy is).

Separate the benefits of your offer by context

Wouldn't it be great if:

- More prospects found you in search

- Your blog posts got hundreds of shares and comments

- People started to recognize your brand

- Your products sold themselves

Blogging Services

More prospects will find you in search and your articles will get hundreds of shares and comments.

Copywriting Services

With engaging copy, your products will sell themselves!

#56: How to spot vague copy and missing information using Google Autotranslate

You may have heard the advice to change the font of your text to spot typos you may have missed the first time.

You can do something similar to spot vague and unclear copy.

If you're multilingual, autotranslate your page into another language you understand. Your brain won't be able to automatically fill in the blanks. Plus, Google Translate doesn't do well with metaphors or fancy wordplays.

So, if the essence of your message got lost in translation, you are being too clever, and your prospects may not have enough information to understand (and appreciate) your offer.

Here's how you can translate your copy with one click.

1) Open translate.google.com.

2) In the first input field, copy-paste:

- A single phrase (for example, your website tagline)

- A URL to translate the whole page

3) Select the language you want to translate it into.

4) Click "translate". If the translation makes you laugh or roll your eyes, rewrite your copy using plain, specific and clear words, then repeat this exercise.

#57: Is using bold font ruining your message?

Quick question: What are highlights on a website?

You probably think they're text in bold font, larger font, a bright button or an image.

Hm. That's actually not what a highlight is. A highlight is something (relatively small) that's different from the (larger) rest.

But when you:

- highlight six lines of text bold
- write five consecutive one-line paragraphs
- enlarge the font of a four-line heading
- or put three buttons next to each other

... there's little left to be different from. There is no 'rest' and, thus, there is no highlight.

Obviously, you need to use them to make your pages scannable and easy to read. But make sure you use highlights on your pages with care and relative to the rest of the content.

Because when everything is bold, nothing is bold. When everything is shiny, nothing is shiny. And when everything looks like a button, nothing looks like a button.

Do this quick exercise.

Open an important sales page on your website and scroll until a spot where you have highlighted text.

How much text on the screen view is *not* highlighted? If it's less than 60%, you know what to do.

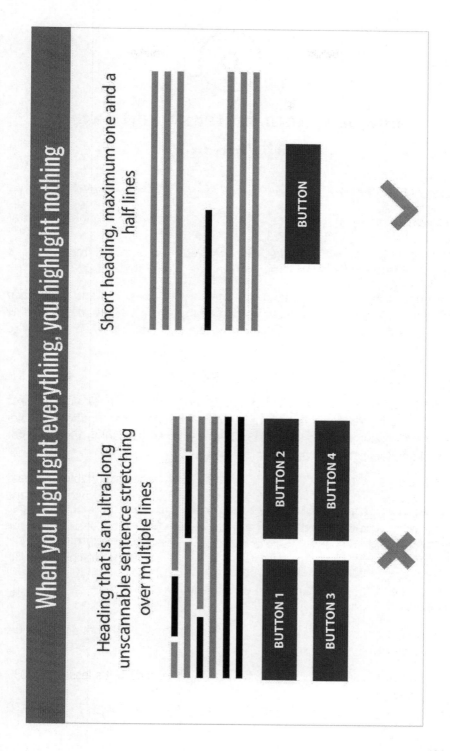

When you highlight everything, you highlight nothing

Short heading, maximum one and a half lines

BUTTON

Heading that is an ultra-long unscannable sentence stretching over multiple lines

BUTTON 1

BUTTON 2

BUTTON 3

BUTTON 4

#58: Why your footer should have a different color

"OMG, seriously, how important is it what color my website footer has?"

#eyeroll

What background color you use for your website footer isn't important. It's important that the color is different from the rest of the page.

When a visitor explores your page, she's trying to understand what each section is about. She expects certain things from a section called "My services" or "About me", and she has certain expectations when it comes to your footer.

But if she fails to recognize the footer, she may:

Not find what she needs: Let's say, she wants to check your returns policy and scrolls down hoping to see it in the footer. Yet, your same-color footer blends in with your page so that she thinks you don't have a footer at all and leaves your website empty-handed.

... or

Waste time looking at something irrelevant: You thought you ended your page with a compelling call to action, but your visitor thinks the page still continues on your same-color footer and scrolls past your CTA.

Make your footer stand out from the rest of the page to make it easier for your visitors to understand your website and find what they're looking for faster.

#59: Your homepage shouldn't mirror your navigation

"Hi there, dear visitor. We are an X company, offering A, B, C. By the way, have you heard that we offer A, B, C?"

This is a conversation you have with your visitors when a part of your homepage mirrors your navigation – offering the same options in the form of a heading + few lines + button with almost as little context as the navigation itself.

Obviously, this isn't the most effective way to use your visitors' time and capitalize on their enthusiasm right after they landed on your homepage.

They've seen your navigation and know the options it offers. Now, they want context.

If you offer services:

- How do these services solve their problems?
- Is there something you specialize in?
- What's your process?
- Why should they trust you?

If you sell products:

- Are there any special offers?
- What are the most popular products?
- Are there any new arrivals?
- Are there any interesting facts or ways to use your products?

Don't waste precious space on your homepage repeating yourself. Instead, offer your visitors context and enticing descriptions of your specific offers to quickly lure them further down your sales funnel.

Don't mirror navigation on your homepage

BUY SELL RENT ABOUT CONTACT

Who we are and what we do

Cars for sale: New offers

VIEW MORE

Cars for rent in your area:

VIEW MORE

BUY SELL RENT ABOUT CONTACT

Who we are and what we do

Buy a car   Sell a car   Rent a car

BUY   SELL   RENT

#60: If your prospects can't imagine it, they won't buy it

Let's do a quick exercise. I'll tell you three things, and you'll try to imagine them.

Ready? Here goes.

Everything.

All your needs.

Any person.

Were you able to imagine anything concrete? No? And neither can your prospects when they read your sales pages with those words in the copy.

For your prospects to get excited about your offer, they need to imagine it. They need to be able to see themselves and / or their problems reflected there.

Not like this:

"We provide a number of services to suit anybody's situation."

"We'll take care of everything for you, looking after all your marketing needs."

But like this:

"We'll walk you through every step of your marketing journey: from building a solid marketing strategy to creating stunning content and running viral campaigns."

Want to sell more? Don't be afraid to write longer copy if it gives your prospects a vivid image they can recognize themselves in. Because if they can't imagine it, they won't buy it.

#61: How to decide the order of the sections on your homepage

Obviously, this question doesn't have a one-size-fits-all answer. However, there are two principles that will help you order the info on your homepage.

#1 Stage of awareness

You need to bridge the gap between what your visitors know about their problems, your offer and the results they want now with what they need to know to convert.

#2 Inverted pyramid

Order the information on your website based on its importance, putting the most important things first.

The following section order provides a good structure to most homepages.

1) What you do / for whom

   - Solopreneurs: Add your photo

   - Ecommerce: Add a CTA button

2) Unique selling point (if not clear from #1)

   - Solopreneurs: "About" section with your unique selling point

3) Credibility enhancers:

   - Testimonials, guarantees, client logos, etc.

4) Overview of your offer(s) with link(s) to dive in:

   - Solopreneurs + agencies: Services

   - Ecommerce: Products

   - Authors: Books

   - Bloggers: Blog posts

5) Credibility enhancers you haven't used in #3 that support claims you make in #4 (for example, case studies)

6) Specific featured aspect(s) of your offer:

- Solopreneurs: Course, lead magnet, book, etc.

- Ecommerce: New products, local offers, etc.

7) Anything else that may nudge your prospects closer towards conversion

How to order the sections on your homepage

What you do / for whom / what's the benefit

Unique selling point (if not clear from above)

Credibility enhancers

- Testimonials
- Social proof
- Guarantees
- Client logos, etc.

Offers overview with links to dive in

- Services
- Product categories
- Books
- Blog posts, etc.

Social proof to support claims from above

Featured offers

- Lead magnet
- Book / course
- Featured service
- Local / new offers, etc.

Rest

- Latest articles
- Events
- FAQs, etc.

#62: How to spot fake benefits in your copy

Benefits are like mushrooms. They may look like something valuable, but if you don't know how to tell them apart, the people you'll be feeding them to won't be thrilled – to put it mildly.

So, how do you spot a fake benefit?

Let's say you're a nutrition coach, and one of your sales pages proudly displays the benefit of your new diet program:

"Flush Deadly Toxins Out of Your Colon!"

But is it really a benefit?

To find that out, ask yourself this question:

Can you imagine your potential client lying awake at night thinking, "Man, I gotta flush some deadly toxins out of my colon!"?

If that image seems rather unlikely to you, congratulations, you've uncovered a fake benefit.

To convert it into a real benefit, ask one simple question: "So what?". And keep asking it until there's no answer.

Here's how.

Flush deadly toxins out of your colon!

So what?

So that your colon is cleansed.

So what?

So that you feel lighter, have more energy and are in a better mood.

Bingo! You've just uncovered a real benefit that you can now include in your copy to make more people relate to it and sign up for your offer.

#63: Don't treat your website like a piece of art

Some people don't have a website. They have a painting.

A splash of this color. A drop of that color. Out-of-space CTAs. And let's not forget a fancy script font, because every modern website needs one of those!

Great to look at but totally dysfunctional.

Your. Website. Is. Not. A. Painting.

Sure, your website shouldn't be ugly. But in the first place, your visitors should be able to:

- Easily recognize what's important
- Read without distractions
- Mentally filter out elements that aren't body text (headings, CTAs)

But what's wrong with using multiple colors, fonts and font sizes?

Well, each different color, font or font size creates friction. Friction is good if you want your visitors to pause and pay attention to that friction-causing thing.

Yet, friction is bad if you want your prospects to read your text attentively without any interruptions.

My recommendation for playing it safe is to use:

- two font families (headings / body text)
- four font sizes (heading / subheading / body text / CTA)
- two colors (body text / headings / CTA) or three if you want to use different colors for headings and body text

... while keeping everything readable (i.e. readable font families, large enough font sizes and colors with good contrast to the background).

Pro tip: If you feel brave, you can use a third font – a readable script font for (very!) short phrases.

Keep the number of different colors and fonts to the minimum

$\mathcal{S}\text{ome}$ IMPORTANT $\mathcal{H}\text{eading}$
Probably important subheading

The most important part of this. Unfortunately, it's difficult to read, because everything else keeps screaming "Look at me!" making it hard for your visitors to concentrate.

A sentence that is actually a CTA >>

SOME IMPORTANT HEADING
Probably important subheading

The most important part of this. Now, it's finally easier to read, because there are fewer colors and fonts, and your visitors are able to understand the purpose of each element faster.

An obvious CTA

#64: Don't waste your time on these popular but useless website tips (and do this instead)

As a small business owner, you don't have the luxury to do things "just to see how it goes".

But how do you know what will work for your website?

Unfortunately, there's no simple answer to this question, as every website is unique. Yet, there are things that you most definitely shouldn't waste your time on.

Here are four popular things you may feel tempted to do, but I urge you not to bother... and do this instead.

1) Customized "Page not found" page

Instead, find and fix broken links (for example, using a free online tool).

2) Customized "Unsubscribe" page

Instead, create a custom "Thank you" page asking your new subscribers to engage with you.

For example, after you thank them for subscribing ask them to do one of these things:

- Fill out a quick survey

- Follow you on a social platform

- Check out one of your popular posts

3) Creative website tagline

Instead, make your website tagline crystal clear and tell your visitors:

- What you do

- Who you do it for

- What the benefit is

4) Fancy website features

Instead, use only website features that support your message and don't add friction or distract your visitors.

#65: Should you display your latest blog posts prominently on your homepage?

Yes. No. Maybe.

It depends on two things:

- The way you earn money from your website
- The goal of your homepage

The general idea is this:

It helps to display the latest blog posts on your homepage ONLY IF 'prospect reading a blog post' is part of your sales funnel. Here's what I mean.

Include the latest blog posts on your homepage if:

- Blogging is the most important part of your business (for example, you're a writer promoting your books or affiliate marketer driving traffic through search).

- You offer services and rely on establishing yourself as an expert to get client inquiries (for example, you're a coach, consultant or copywriter), and the majority of your blog posts are really good.

- Your sales funnel starts with getting people on your list, which often happens after they read a blog post.

Don't include the latest blog posts on your homepage if:

- Most people come to your website with a strong intention to buy (for example, if you run an online store).

- You need to explain a lot about your offer on your homepage and including the latest blog posts doesn't fit the homepage 'story'.

- You have a total of four blog posts over the last two years.

- Your blog posts suck, to be honest.

#66: The most effective tip that will make any website faster

Ready? Here goes:

> **Don't put so much junk on your website!**

Every image, every fancy feature, every new font you add to your website slows it down.

Before adding anything to your website, ask yourself:

- What did my visitors come to this page for?
- Why do I want this thing on my page: because it makes my message stronger or because it looks fancy?
- Will this element or feature pull my visitors' attention in the wrong direction?
- Will this thing annoy them or interrupt their train of thought?

Get rid of the things that don't add value:

- Things that move by themselves (for example, blog post, testimonial and client logo carousels)
- Decorative images that don't contribute to the main goal of the page
- Background images where no background or a color background will also do
- GIFs, unless they explain something faster than words
- Embedded feeds from social networks (Facebook, Twitter, Pinterest, etc.), unless you get a lot of business from them

#67: An ultra-effective way to make more subscribers open your email newsletters

You probably think I'm going to talk about email subject lines.

Nope.

Ensuring that more subscribers open your emails starts long before you send out your first newsletter.

It starts with a "Thank you for subscribing" page.

Do you have a custom "thank you" page? If not, you can create one by specifying the URL of the page in your email marketing software.

You'll find it within the settings for a sign-up form under *Confirmation Thank You Page* or just *Thank You Page*.

But don't just make it say "Thank you for subscribing". Add a prominent call to action to extend the interaction between you and your new subscribers.

For example:

- Embed a one-question survey that will help you learn more about your new subscribers
- Ask them to follow you on a specific social platform
- Encourage them to check out your popular posts

How will this help increase your email open rates?

Because of a longer interaction, your new subscribers will be more likely to remember your name and have positive associations with it (and, thus, be more likely to open your next email when it lands in their inbox).

Think of how many times you deleted an email without reading it because you didn't remember subscribing and didn't recognize the sender.

Exactly!

How to use your "thank you" page effectively

Great, thanks!

Your checklist is on its way. Check your email in a minute.

} Reminder to check their email

By the way, are you on Twitter?

▼ Attention-grabbing line

If you are, let's connect! I tweet snackable tips around website improvements and occasionally rant about bad website copy.

} Expectations / benefit

Follow Gill on Twitter

▼ Prominent call to action

} Your photo

#68: Want more people to click on your CTA button? Avoid a false bottom

So, you have a visually prominent call to action on your page. "Contact me". "Download ebook". "Register for the webinar".

Why aren't your visitors clicking it then?

Here are just three of many possible reasons:

1) You're asking them to click on your button before giving them enough info to want to do that.

2) Your page has a false bottom – an area on your page that looks like it's the end of the page, although there is still content below, including your CTA button (see the image at the end of this chapter).

3) #1 plus your false bottom hides important copy that was supposed to persuade them to click.

Re #1: Obviously, you can't expect your prospects to click "Contact me" before you tell them about your services. So, you need to make sure your CTA button doesn't come too early.

Re #2 and #3: Make sure you don't have an area on your page that your visitors may mistake for its end. The feeling of the 'end of page' intensifies if you have a false bottom right after a CTA.

This can happen on any page – sales pages and blog posts. The example on the next page illustrates a false bottom in a blog post.

Want your visitors to read the whole page? Avoid a false bottom.

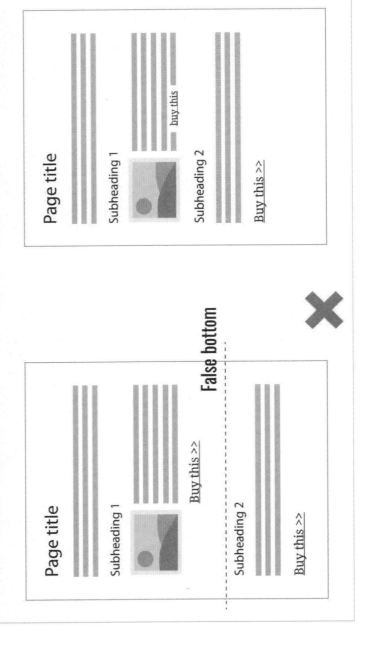

#69: How to present categories and tags on your website (and keep visitors exploring your content)

How are you presenting tags and categories on your website?

Let me guess: somewhere at the end of your posts in small gray letters, right? No wonder your visitors don't use them!

Here's how to present tags and categories so that your visitors also see and use them.

1) Make sure you have a clear website tagline that tells your visitors what your website is about, and a descriptive navigation.

   What does this have to do with tags and categories?

   If your visitors don't understand what you do or can't easily find your Blog page, they won't care about or even look at your tags and categories.

2) Organize your content in categories and tags properly:

   • Make sure all your categories contain an approximately equal amount of posts (i.e. are of a similar size).

   • If you have a category that is twice as large as the rest, split it in half.

   • Don't assign too many categories or tags to one post.

   • If you use a tag or a category only once or twice, remove it.

3) Make sure your visitors see a page title and a short description on all category and tag pages.

4) Present your tags early on the page, before the posts.

But what's the **difference between a category and a tag** anyway?

You can think of categories as the table of contents for your website. These are the 'chapter titles' that can also have 'sub-chapters' (i.e. a hierarchy).

Your tags are like the index. They don't have a hierarchy and refer to something much more specific than categories.

Do you have to use both?

You don't have to use either. Yet, categories and tags help your website visitors discover more content that's similar to what they've just read or that covers a particular topic they're interested in. Plus, category and tag pages may rank in search, so if you use them properly, you can only win.

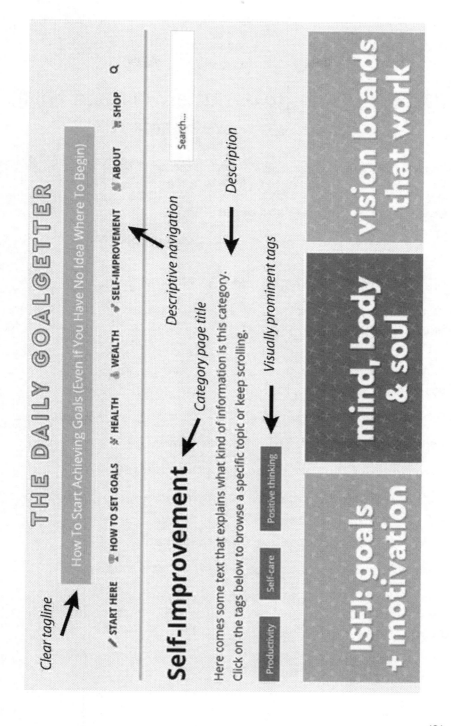

Clear tagline

THE DAILY GOALGETTER

How To Start Achieving Goals (Even if You Have No Idea Where To Begin)

✎ START HERE ♟ HOW TO SET GOALS ⚡ HEALTH ⚖ WEALTH ✈ SELF-IMPROVEMENT ⚙ ABOUT 🛒 SHOP ⚲

Search...

Descriptive navigation

Description

Self-Improvement

Category page title

Here comes some text that explains what kind of information is this category.
Click on the tags below to browse a specific topic or keep scrolling.

Visually prominent tags

Productivity   Self-care   Positive thinking

ISFJ: goals + motivation

mind, body & soul

vision boards that work

131

#70: Eight steps to declutter your homepage (and win more business)

You know your homepage needs a revamp but don't know where to begin? Follow these steps to get through it without feeling overwhelmed.

Step #1: Start with pen and paper

Close all browser tabs. Take a pen and a piece of paper and forget what's currently on your website.

Step #2: Write your header text (quickly)

Write down a tagline that is clear and relevant for your target audience. Nothing creative. Just a couple of clear words regarding what you do, for whom and how it helps.

Then, add one to two sentences to give your prospects a better idea of what you do and why they should care.

Step #3: Add navigation labels

Add clear and descriptive navigation labels. Avoid drop-down menus.

Step #4: Decide on the purpose of your homepage

For this, complete the sentence: *"Ideally, I want a prospect who visits my homepage to...".*

Step #5: Decide what subsections to include

Decide what your prospects need to hear (not what you want to say).

What do your prospects know about their problems and your solution? How do they feel? What do they need to know / feel to check out other main pages on your website?

Think in terms of the subsections and write down their titles (for now, in no particular order).

Step #6: Organize the subsections

Organize the subsections based on the inverted pyramid principle, putting the most important information first.

Step #7: Add CTAs

Based on the page's purpose (#4), add relevant CTA buttons. See Chapter #19, page 34 if you need help with that.

Step #8: Compare your sketch to your current page

What's the most important difference?

I'm willing to bet that your sketch has more white space and fewer visual elements.

And that's exactly how your website should be. Only the things that are necessary to help your visitors reach their goals (and, thus, help you reach yours) belong on your website. Not a word, a color or an image more.

#71: Feeling stuck working on your website tagline? Try this

I was once asked to write a homepage header section: the main headline and subheadline.

Seems easy, right?

But when I checked out the company's website, I got nervous. They listed a gazillion features! What should be the first thing their visitors learn about their product?

Finally, I got an idea.

I can't tell you exactly what that company did. Let's say they sold teleportation devices (and pretend nobody knows what a teleportation device is).

So, in a nutshell, the copy I came up with was this:

The fastest possible way to get from A to B

Forget traffic jams, messed up train schedules and exhausting flights.
Get where you need to be in seconds.

The logic behind these three sentences is the following:

{Unique feature that differentiates you from competition}

{Main problem of customers + solution your product
offers for it}

Not very creative? Maybe. Clear and specific? For sure! Because now everyone understands what a teleportation device does and what benefits it has.

#missionaccomplished

Try this formula next time you need to write (or rewrite) a homepage header section.

#72: A surefire way to find out if your new blog post is any good

So, you wrote a new post. Congrats. Now, let's see if it's any good.

Scroll through it reading just the section headings.

Is it still worthwhile for your visitors to read the actual text? Or can they learn everything there is to learn just from those seven bold lines?

If it's the latter, I have bad news. You just wrote the "X obvious things about Y everyone knows already (but hey, it's beautifully formatted)" post.

Clear section headings are a good thing. But if they give away everything there is to know about your article, then there wasn't much value in it in the first place. And there's no point reading the rest.

Unless you're famous and people share your beautifully formatted articles without reading them, your readers won't share or comment on your newest creation.

What to do instead?

- Make sure you aren't repeating what everybody else has been saying and add your own perspective
- Look at the topic from an unexpected angle
- Add a twist in the headings, still keeping them clear
- Add humor and personality

Can't do that? Select a different topic for your post. Otherwise, your visitors will 'drive through' your post like it's a motorway without remembering you or your website.

(D)

#73: Want more conversions? Remove the noise around your CTAs (real-life example)

I posted something on LinkedIn once and got a comment from Michael Pozdnev, a blogger. He told me that he followed my advice and shared a screenshot of a page on his website.

It was a "Thank you for subscribing" page where he embedded a one-question survey hoping for responses.

Although it wasn't the topic of my post, I couldn't (yet again) keep myself from giving unsolicited advice.

I told Michael:

... that the page had too many visual highlights and calls to action (download guide, survey, social buttons, etc.)

... and that whatever he wants his new subscribers to do, they'll be more likely to do it if it's the only CTA on the page.

Plus, that the field for the comment should look like a proper input field and not some divider, but that's a different story.

Michael got straight to work.

And what do you know?

After just 11 days, the updated page got him as many survey responses as his old page did in 4.5 months (!).

Later, he wrote to me again saying his conversion rate jumped from 6.3% to 27.9% (sample size: 887 conversions).

Bottom line: Want more conversions? Remove the visual noise around your main CTA.

Remove the visual noise around your CTAs to increase conversion

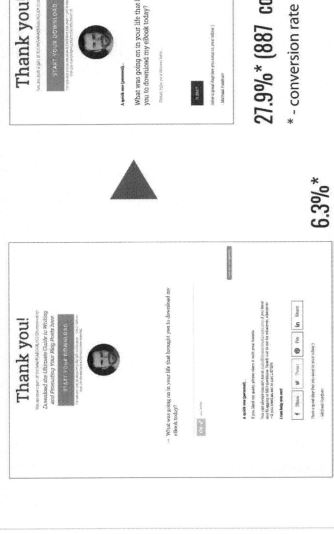

6.3%*

27.9%* (887 conversions)

* - conversion rate

#74: How to choose the right words to call your products and services

I get asked this a lot.

Should we call our new offer "marketing courses" or "marketing training"?

Should we call our lotion "after sun" or "post sunscreen"?

My answer is always the same: My opinion doesn't matter and neither does yours.

What matters is what your target audience calls the solution to their problems (aka your product / services).

Do they think, "I'd like to go on some marketing training" or "I think I need to join a marketing course"?

"Great, Gill. And how am I supposed to know that? I can't read their minds, can I?"

Yes, you can. Just do keyword research and check which phrase has a higher search volume.

When your product is new or there's not a big enough search volume to rely on, check out Amazon reviews or forums to uncover common phrases your target audience uses when talking about their problems / solutions they need.

Or imagine them talking about their problem to a friend.

Do they think, "I need an after sun lotion to soothe my irritated skin" or "I need a post sunscreen lotion"?

Usually, a phrase that sounds more natural is a better choice.

Using the exact same words as your target audience is the key to persuasive copy that resonates.

#75: Want to know if your website visitors like your content and offers? Watch session replays

Did you know that you can record videos that show how your visitors interact with your web pages?

It may seem a bit creepy, because it feels like you're looking over your visitors' shoulder, but session recordings are totally legal and indispensable if you want to know what your visitors *really* think of your content and offers.

To record user sessions, you'll need a 3rd party tool. I use a free plan from HotJar, but there are plenty of alternatives.

Just go to their website, create an account and follow the installation instructions.

Pay special attention to the sessions on your:

- Homepage
- Important sales pages
- Pages with a lead magnet

Use session recordings to discover:

- Design issues that appear only on particular devices (for example, iPads or Mac PCs with ridiculously large resolution)
- Where your users pause and read attentively
- Which sections of your page they don't notice and quickly scroll past
- Where they click (and whether those links are working)
- Pages that don't meet user intent (session duration 0-10 seconds)
- Pages that your visitors love (session duration over one minute while active)

#76: Why you should remove even minor annoyances from your website

Will a visitor leave your website if you don't have a "Home" navigation label? Probably not.

And if you have a long drop-down menu? This is also usually no biggie (yet).

Testimonial carousels? Slightly annoying, but nah.

But what if you have *all* of those things plus a couple of other minor annoyances?

Then a large pile of straw on the camel's back is growing, and any additional straw may break its back anytime.

Here are some common annoyances you should consider fixing on your website:

- No "Home" navigation label
- Many / long drop-down menus in the navigation
- Stuff that moves by itself (carousels, extensive animations, GIFs, etc.)
- Autoplay audio / video
- Pop-ups, slide-ups, welcome mats
- Unclear copy on navigation labels and buttons
- Social media icons or a banner that doesn't move when you scroll (aka "sticky banner") that partially covers the text
- Sticky banner occupying half of the screen

The majority of the issues listed above don't affect readability. Your visitors can still see and read your text. But they'll get slightly irritated by each of these things until they have enough and leave your website.

#77: How to spot sloppy website design

This tip has been brought to you by a web designer who was in charge of implementing the mockups I once designed for my client.

Is this how your website looks, too?

Modern fonts, lots of white space, nice color palette, hip section separators.

Looks fancy, one may think. Except that it's not.

Because:

- different sizes for body font
- different amount of white space between the lines of the same paragraphs
- more white space between related than unrelated elements
- unequal amount of white space between the last element of the section, section separation line and the first element of the next section

...make your design look messy and unprofessional.

"Ah, but my website visitors don't care about that. They aren't some web design nerds!"

They may not care but their subconscience does.

Our brain loves symmetry and balance in design and hates disproportion and chaos.

Your visitors won't be able to put their finger on it, but they won't perceive your website (or you) as professional either.

Now, open your website. How many of these web design 'sins' do you see?

How to spot sloppy web design

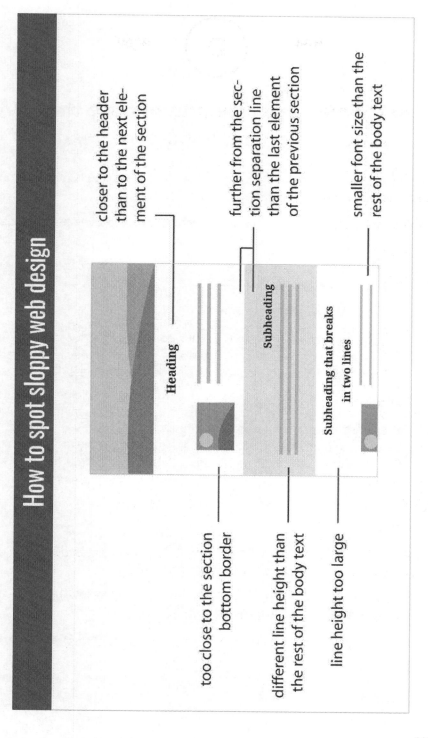

#78: Why you may want to remove that CTA button from your homepage header

I think the most challenging thing to achieve on a web page is to make your visitors read the info in the order you want them to.

That's why I treat every button with caution: because it gives people a way out of my carefully laid out conversation.

Enter a call-to-action button above the fold on your homepage, the most typical being "Contact me".

Here's why you may want to remove it.

Since most of the people who land on your homepage see it (and you) for the first time, your button is asking them to do something they aren't ready to do yet (to contact you). Which means that button is useless.

But could you leave it just in case?

Well, there are also people who click a button "just because it's there", despite not being ready to contact you. And this interrupts the order in which you wanted them to read your homepage.

Still want a button above the fold?

Do it if:

- You're famous (then, just do whatever you want)

- You're SaaS (a suitable CTA: "Start free trial")

- You have many repeat visitors, and the button lets them do an important task (a suitable CTA: "Log in")

- Your offer is simple, and your button leads to a "Services" page (for example, if you're a copywriter)

- The space above the fold on your website is featuring a lead magnet (suitable CTAs: "Take the quiz", "Download my ebook")

#79: Don't try too hard to make your prospects like you

You know how sometimes you desperately want someone to like you but say things that have an opposite effect?

About that...

Exhibit A:

"We're hard-working, pragmatic and think big."

Imagine, a stranger rang your doorbell and introduced himself as the world's most successful business coach. Would you believe him?

Your prospects won't believe those self-serving adjectives either.

Want to appear likable AND trustworthy? Use clear words and be specific while describing things they care about. For example, your process:

"We start every project by involving the most experienced members of our team until things are streamlined and can be carefully delegated back to you."

Exhibit B:

"Bob Johnson, Project Manager. Life motto: Work smart, not hard. Passionate about overcoming challenges and coffee."

Your prospects are selfish. They don't care about your motto or passions. All they care about is how / if you can solve their problems. And they certainly don't care about your beverage preferences.

Want to appear likable AND trustworthy while talking about your team? Show how your team members can solve a relevant problem:

"Bob Johnson, Project Manager. 15 years' experience with international projects. Masterfully navigates the ever-changing project requirements."

#80: Speak directly to your prospects to make it easier for them to relate to what you're saying

Imagine this.

Your boss called for a team meeting, and she isn't happy. She says, "Some individuals embarrassed our client."

You think, "Eh, whatever. Some individuals, not me."

But what if she says, "You embarrassed our client."

Suddenly, you're paying attention. Although she uses "you" to mean "all of you", your stress levels shoot up as you feel like she's speaking directly to you.

Same with your copy.

Except you shouldn't scare your prospects but say nice things — like describing their problems or benefits of your offer — addressing them directly.

Not like this:

- "The locking tilt-in-space function makes it easier for **individuals** to sit in comfort and safety."

- "I provide this service for **business owners** who need a plan for the next stage of business growth."

But like this:

- "The locking tilt-in-space function makes it easier for **you**..."

- "**Need** a plan to take **your** business to the next stage? **Get** [these awesome things that will make your life easier like that]."

Address your prospects with "you". Let them feel like you're speaking directly to them, and it will get their fingers to press the "buy" button faster.

Speak directly to your prospects

YOU

▲▲ ▲

Individuals

Business owners

Users

Population, etc.

"The locking tilt-in-space function makes it easier for users to sit in comfort and safety."

"The locking tilt-in-space function makes it easier for you to sit in comfort and safety."

#81: Are you being a wuss? Use assertive language to appear confident

Are you a cat or a dog person?

I'm team cat. I'm afraid of dogs, and it's a vicious circle because I can see them sensing my fear, which makes me even more scared.

Your prospects are like dogs.

They sense when you're afraid. Afraid that you aren't good enough. And although they won't bite, if you say stuff like this on your website, they won't get in touch with you either:

"Feel free to reach out in case you're interested in a discussion about your brand's web content."

Maybe.

Perhaps.

Possibly.

In case you're interested.

Burn these with fire and substitute them with assertive language:

- Feel free to reach out => Contact me

- In case you're interested => Interested? Contact me OR [Want this benefit]? Contact me

- Perhaps we can work together => Let's work together

- Maybe we're a good fit => Add a section "Who is this service for?" where you describe who'll benefit from your services most

Because if you aren't sure you're any good, how can your prospects be sure? And even if you're suffering from imposter syndrome, your prospects don't have to know.

#82: Here's what it takes to convert strangers into customers

Have you thought about it? What do you think needs to happen for someone who's never heard of you or your website to buy from you?

At a high level, for a stranger to become a customer, they'd need to:

1) Find their way to your website

2) Get a good first impression and their initial question answered

3) Easily discover more relevant quality content

4) Trust you

5) Be convinced to buy and easily purchase when they're ready

"Oh, just five steps then!"

If you think it's simple, look at this part:

Easily discover more relevant quality content.

Fulfilling the promise of these six words is hard work that includes:

- Flawless user experience
- Clear navigation
- Internal links
- Many quality posts and email newsletters

Enough to get your head spinning, huh.

I wish I could tell you there's a quick and easy solution to this, but creating a website that drives business requires work. Yet, the sooner you start doing it, the better.

So, if you still don't have a plan of how you're going to attract new business, look at the image on the next page.

Is there something you need to pay more attention to?

If you need more details about which steps to take, this checklist will help: **gillandrews.com/website-checklist-pdf**.

What it takes to convert strangers into customers

Be convinced to buy	Sales pages, Conversion process
Trust you	Social proof
Discover more relevant content	Site structure, Blog, Newsletter
Get good 1st impression / Get their Qs answered	Load speed, Design & formatting, Content quality
Find their way to your website	SEO, Social media, Networking, Ads

Get to know, like and trust you

#83: Convert more prospects by answering the right mini questions

When your prospects are browsing your website, they have an endless flow of questions. Not only the fundamental questions that keep them awake at night, but also many mini questions in the context of what they see on your website.

What is this?

How does this work?

Can I trust this person?

I'm ready to buy. What now?

With every click and scroll, they're trying to get those questions answered.

Want to know how to convert more prospects into customers? Anticipate their mental state and answer their mini questions.

Here's how.

1) For every page / page section, think what mini questions your prospects could be asking. For example:

   • At the beginning of a homepage or a landing page, it's "What is it?"

   • On About page, "How can I learn more about this?"

   • On a Contact page, "I'm ready to contact her. How can I do that?"

2) Now, answer these mini questions. The matrix on the next page shows you how. As you can see, not every page or page section requires you to say a lot.

   For example, don't start answering questions about your offer before you tell them what it is.

And there's also no need to reiterate the benefits of your offer on the Contact page – a prospect who clicked on your "Contact" link and landed there is already convinced.

3) Regardless of the page, make sure your copy is clear, relevant and valuable, and that the design doesn't get in the way.

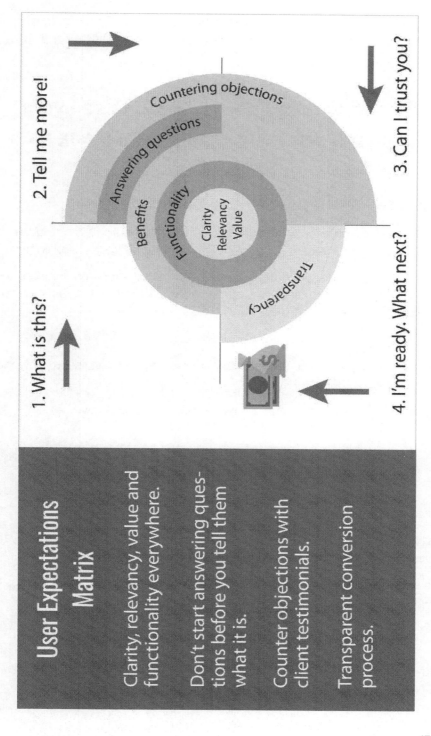

User Expectations Matrix

Clarity, relevancy, value and functionality everywhere.

Don't start answering questions before you tell them what it is.

Counter objections with client testimonials.

Transparent conversion process.

1. What is this?

2. Tell me more!

3. Can I trust you?

4. I'm ready. What next?

Countering objections

Answering questions

Benefits

Functionality

Clarity
Relevancy
Value

Transparency

#84: How many people need to see your opt-in pop-up before you get one engaged subscriber?

1,319. Yup, one thousand three hundred and bloody nineteen.

This is how many people, on average, need to see an opt-in pop-up on a small or medium business website for you to get an engaged subscriber.

It's easy to fall for all those case studies that show pop-ups work for websites with tons of traffic and faceless business models. But these big websites can pay the price that comes with it.

You as a small business owner? Most probably not.

How many potential clients need to see your pop-up for you to get one engaged subscriber?

Use this formula to find out a specific number for your own website:[*]

$$\frac{100}{\text{Pop-up conversion rate (\%)}} \times \frac{100}{\text{Email click-through rate (\%)}}$$

Example:

Let's say your email click-through rate is 10%. You don't have a pop-up yet, so let's take the average 3% conversion rate.

To get one subscriber that clicks on the links in your email newsletters, you'll need to show your pop-up to:

$$\frac{100}{3} \times \frac{100}{10} = \text{about 333 website visitors}$$

Now that you've calculated this number, do you think it's worth potentially alienating that many prospects just to get one engaged subscriber?

Maybe it is, maybe it isn't. You decide.

But how can you grow your list without any interstitials?

Here are four ways:

- Use a sticky header with an offer that goes beyond a free ebook
- Use a sticky footer with a sign-up form and a compelling message
- Use a "subscribe" button strategically placed within exceptional content
- Create a dedicated page for your lead magnet and make it rank in search

* – If you're curious where this formula comes from, check out an article on my website Gillandrews.com called *"Unexpected Pop-up Statistics: The #1 Reason to Ditch Pop-up Forms"*.

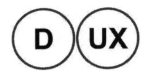

#85: The more elements you have on a web page, the less attention each element gets

Tell me this: Do you think your visitors are blind? Or stupid? Or a goldfish?

So why on earth are you bombarding them with huge "Contact me", "Call us" and "Download this" buttons as if you're afraid the moment a button disappears from view they'll forget it exists?

The image at the end of this chapter shows a page I once reviewed almost exactly as it was, and it's not untypical. I was asked to make the page more user-friendly, and my suggestion was this:

Leave your visitors in peace.

Let them read the article they came to you for without screaming your own agenda at them.

Sure, you want them to contact you. So, let them know it's an option – once in the navigation (for all the pages) and once as a sticky element (for this particular page in the sidebar).

This way:

- Your visitors will notice your buttons, because there are just two CTAs with lots of white space around them.

- They won't feel pressured, because the way the CTAs are presented feels less like an ad and more like a helpful reminder.

And don't worry. They'll remember where to find that button when they need it.

The more you show, the less attention each element gets

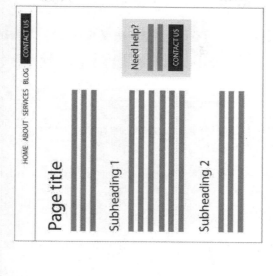

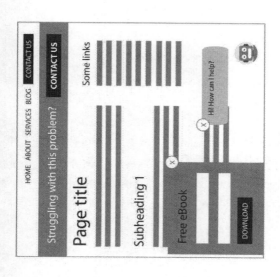

#86: The more complex your topic, the simpler your design needs to be

Color backgrounds. Separation lines. Icons.

All good ideas that can improve the reading experience in one case and complicate your visitor's life in another.

Why? Because of the cognitive load – the brain power your visitors need to use to process your page.

The more complex your topic,

... the more brain power your visitors need to spend to understand your words,

... the less capacity they have to process your design without feeling overwhelmed.

Things that add to cognitive load (among others) are:

- Long paragraphs
- Different font sizes and families
- Complex shapes
- Every additional color
- Separation lines
- Complex graphics or icons

Obviously, stripping your article of any highlights will make it visually monotonous and difficult to process.

So, what's the compromise?

- Unify your styling as much as possible:

- Use the same section structure and styling describing similar things (your services, different things that belong to the same category, etc.)
- Use the same font family and size for headings of the same level
- Don't use different elements for the same purpose (or the same elements for different purposes)
- Use as few visual highlights on one screen view as possible
- Use shorter paragraphs
- Use white space between individual bullet points

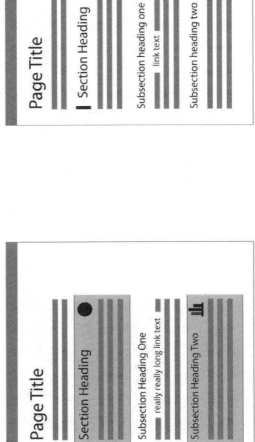

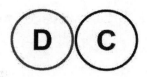

#87: Want more client inquiries? Make your Contact page more human

Have you slapped a contact form on your Contact page and called it a day?

Oh, you also listed your email address and your phone number!

That... still doesn't make it any better.

If you want more people to contact you, you need to do better than a generic form.

Effective Contact page 'must-haves':

- Your photo / a photo of someone from your customer services + a friendly paragraph of text in a conversational tone
- A mention of how long it usually takes you to respond to inquiries
- A contact form instead (or along with) an email address

Having a contact form also allows you to:

- Ask for particular information in advance
- Track submissions
- Reduce the number of spam emails
- Add a "thank you" page

Other info to include on your Contact page (if applicable):

- Phone number
- Office hours
- Map and driving directions

Don't forget to link to your Contact page from:

- Main navigation
- Individual service pages
- Footer

Make your Contact page more "human"

√ Your photo

√ A friendly paragraph of text in a conversational tone

√ Mention how soon you usually respond

√ Use a contact form (not just email address)

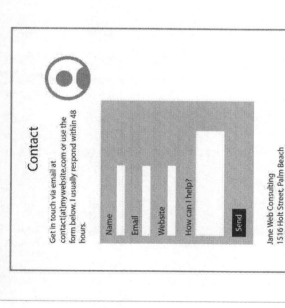

Contact

Get in touch via email at contact(at)mywebsite.com or use the form below. I usually respond within 48 hours.

Name

Email

Website

How can I help?

Send

Jane Web Consulting
1516 Holt Street, Palm Beach
FL 33401

#88: Comparing your website to other websites? Here's how to do it right

Sometimes I ask a client why they have a certain element on their page, and they say it's because all these other websites have it, too.

A valid argument?

Consider this example: Many studies show that carousels don't work. In particular, website visitors fail to absorb the info they present. But Amazon.com has a carousel!

Sure, but Amazon:

- Doesn't need to explain what it does
- Has millions of returning visitors who know how the site works
- Uses the carousel as an ad banner for new offers

And you:

- Need to explain what you do
- Have many new visitors who've never heard of you
- Use your carousel to communicate important things, like your value proposition

See my point?

You should only compare your website to websites that:

- Are in the same niche
- Belong to a business of the same size
- Have a similar target audience and business model
- Solve similar problems

Plus, be clear about the reasons why you want that thing on your website.

A good reason not to compare at all: You can't be sure other website owners know what they're doing.

But your chances of winning valuable insights are higher if you look at websites with high traffic that are a couple of steps ahead of you. The owners of those websites usually A/B test things, so their website choices are based on data and reflect the real preferences of their target audience.

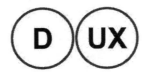

#89: Five ways you're unintentionally hiding important info from your prospects

Getting stuff right on your website is like cooking a perfect soft-boiled egg. It's easier to screw it up than get it right, and even experienced cooks fail at times.

Below, you'll find five examples of bad web design that hides important information from your website visitors.

1) Text that appears on hover

Not everyone will guess that they need to hover over an icon to see some additional info. Plus, screen readers ignore the text that appears on hover and hover effects don't work on mobile.

So, make the important info visible right away.

2) Tabs

The image at the end of this chapter shows a typical tab layout. Not everyone will realize that there are clickable tabs on your page that contain additional information. And even if they do, not everyone will make an extra effort to click on them.

So, display the info right away in the subsequent sections.

3) Text links on sales pages

Don't send a visitor to another page to learn something important to the current conversation. Not everyone will find that important info on a totally different page and not everyone will come back.

So, summarize what you expect your visitors to learn from that other page on the current page. This way, you won't interrupt the reading flow and won't risk a bounce.

4) Links that look like plain text

If it's not clear that an element is clickable, fewer people will click on it.

So, make links look like buttons, text in a contrasting color or underlined text (see also Chapter #10, page 21).

5) Slider / carousel

In case you missed the other ten times I mentioned it already: Carousels fail to communicate important info as they rotate too fast.

So, use a static image plus text or A/B test your carousel to make sure it indeed performs better than a static image.

Bottom line: Have something important to say to your prospects? Make it static. Make it visible. Make it noticeable.

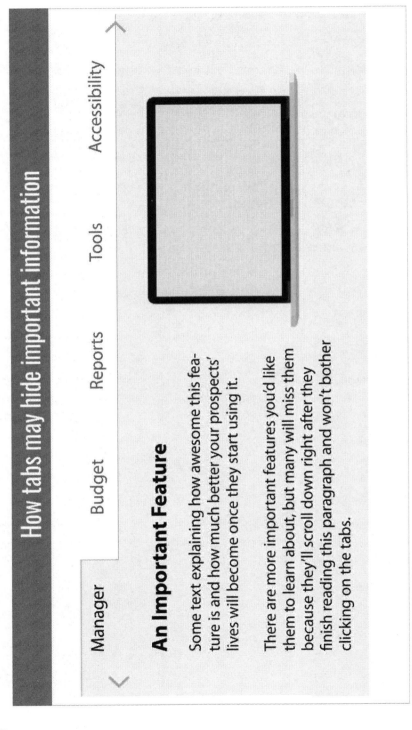

How tabs may hide important information

Manager Budget Reports Tools Accessibility

An Important Feature

Some text explaining how awesome this feature is and how much better your prospects' lives will become once they start using it.

There are more important features you'd like them to learn about, but many will miss them because they'll scroll down right after they finish reading this paragraph and won't bother clicking on the tabs.

#90: To get more people to read your blog posts, go beyond a standard Blog page

What does your Blog page look like?

It's probably just several columns of your latest posts, right?

But what if your latest posts don't resonate with a particular visitor? Then she's likely to leave without reading anything.

Here are three ways to supercharge your Blog page and encourage more people to read your blog posts.

1) Add a Blog focus, featured posts and a sign-up form

- At the top of your Blog page, add one to two sentences telling your readers what you blog about.

- Feature the posts you want more people to see next to each other in a row so that your readers can see more posts without scrolling (for example, your most popular posts or posts containing lead magnets).

- Add a sign-up form to get new subscribers (and more people who'll visit your Blog when you publish a new blog post).

2) Add featured topics

- Before those columns of latest blog posts, list several post categories offering your readers an opportunity to jump to a topic of interest right away.

3) Categorize everything

- Offer your readers a complete overview of your posts organized by topic.

Your Blog page is one of the most visited pages on your website. Go beyond a standard layout and offer your website visitors a better way to discover relevant content.

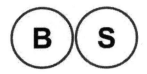

#91: How to get more comments on your blog posts

You might've heard this advice already:

To get more comments, ask people to comment in the final paragraph of your blog post (for example, in an "Over to you" section). Or add your own comment asking a question that aims to start a discussion.

All great tips... that won't work if you get the following wrong.

Does your comment section come right after your final paragraph, clearly visible to your readers?

Or is it an afterthought that comes after your opt-in, "share this" icons and the related articles section?

Because once they finish reading your blog post, your readers are about to leave. And unless you show them your comment section quickly, they may assume you don't have one.

To clarify: There's nothing wrong with putting an opt-in at the end of a post. But it's a question of priorities. Whatever comes first gets more attention.

Putting an opt-in first may get you more subscribers. Putting related articles first may get people to read more of your blog posts.

Maybe that's your goal, and you don't care about the comments at all. But if your empty comment section makes you sad, you know what to do.

How to get more comments on your blog posts

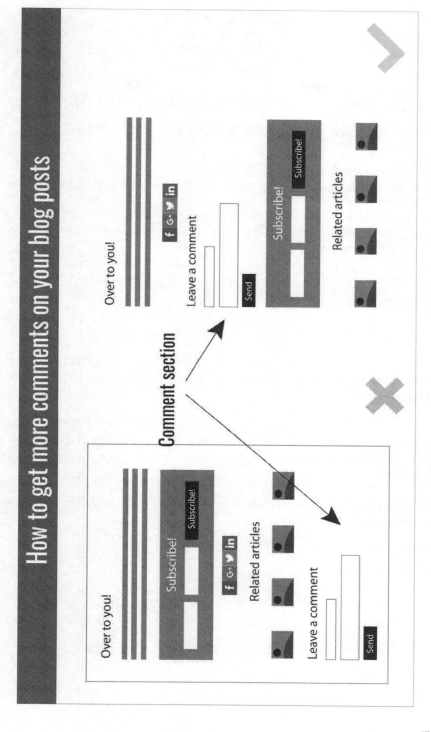

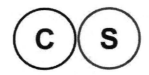

#92: Why a contractor who can't spell is sometimes a better copywriter than you

When he sent me an inquiry full of typos, I thought nothing good could come out of this. But I replied, and what followed was a great lesson.

Jim was a contractor running a family-owned business. He wanted me to review his website. He wrote the copy himself, so I was prepared for the worst when I checked it out.

But, boy, was I wrong.

Sure, the copy was wordy, had typos and was full of never-ending paragraphs. But what was happening on his website was a valuable conversation.

He asked questions, mentioned real benefits and empathized with his prospects the way only a person who knows his business and clients inside out could do.

And here's where Jim is better than many copywriters out there: He knows his product and he knows what his clients need. Not from some generic niche research, but because he's been doing it for 18 years. You can't quickly google that.

So, before you apply all that AIDA*-shmaida or some quick tips and tricks, ask yourself:

What is this?

- How is it being sold?
- Why should people buy it?
- Who'll benefit most from it?
- What criteria do people use to make a buying decision?
- What reservations / objections might they have?

Otherwise, your copy will have so many holes that no AIDA can patch them.

* – AIDA is a copywriting formula that stands for "Attention, Interest, Desire, Action" and is often used in marketing and advertising.

#93: Don't organize your website like it's a department store

In a department store, everything is organized in sections.

Burger buns are in the bread section, M&M's in the sweets department, and you usually won't find pickles on the same shelf as cereal.

Some freelancers and knowledge-based businesses treat their websites the same way:

- Info about themselves only on the "About" page
- Services only on the "Services" page
- Testimonials only on the "Testimonials" page

Everything's so nicely compartmentalized, a department store would be proud.

But a store:

- Doesn't know what products an average customer needs, so mixing stuff together won't make sense
- Can afford to have customers spend a bit more time searching for products, because going to another store will take them much longer than those extra three minutes they need to find the peanut butter

Yet, you:

- (Should) know your customers' exact needs and can mix your 'products' (aka pieces of information) to match those needs faster
- Can't afford to make them wander along your 'aisles' for too long searching for the right info, because your competitor is just a click away

Plus, persuasion is best done in a conversation where nobody needs to run to another 'section' to get the missing piece of info.

Which means:

- On your homepage, include some info about you, your services and social proof

- On every sales page, include testimonials

- On your "About" page, talk not only about yourself but also how you help

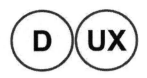

#94: Make sure your text has the right contrast ratio to be easy to read

How ironic is that: You've been obsessing over your tagline, header image and page copy but have never checked if people can actually read them with ease.

Given all the overlays, color backgrounds and text on images your website theme allows you to use, it's easy to forget that readability comes first.

And what is 'readable' anyway?

Luckily, there's an objective answer to that called "contrast ratio".

It's defined within Web Content Accessibility Guidelines (now say it fast three times in a row) and measures the difference in perceived brightness between two colors – foreground and background.

Aim for contrast ratio over 4.5:1 for normal and 7:1 for large text.

Don't trust your website theme default colors (I've seen default settings fail this test many times).

Check the contrast ratio for your text and background using a free online tool called *Color Contrast Checker*.

To find out what colors your website uses, install a free browser plug-in called *ColorZilla*. It lets you find out any color of any website element, be it text, background or image, just by hovering over it.

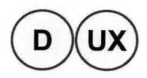

#95: Why your website should be 80% like everyone else's

Your website won't be the first ever website your prospects see in their lives. Moreover, it won't be the first website they see *in your niche*.

For example, when they think "copywriter", they already have a mental image of what a copywriter's website should look like.

This is called *prototypicality* – a mental image your brain creates to categorize stuff. If something is prototypical (i.e. matches the mental image people have for this category), it's easier to understand and use.

Which means, if your website has a look and a structure similar to other websites in your niche, your visitors will have less trouble using it. Plus, prototypical feels familiar, and familiarity evokes trust.

Not sure what's prototypical for your niche? Check out your competitors' websites and note:

- How many colors / what color palettes they use
- How many / what labels are in the navigation
- How's the homepage structured
- Do they use real photos, etc.

It's possible that your visitors expect things from your website that it's not providing. Or, if it looks too different, they don't feel like they can trust you.

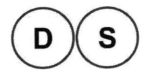

#96: When it's better to have two website navigation menus

When you started your business, your navigation was just Home, About, Services, Contact.

But now you've written books, created courses and started offering more services. And you want your prospects to know about them.

One problem: If you link to all of that in the navigation menu, it will explode.

Here's a solution: Use two main navigation menus.

Let's say you're thinking of including these labels in your main navigation: Home, About, Services, Case Studies, Courses, Book, Blog, Contact.

Notice how those labels can be separated into two categories:

- Sales pages where your prospects can learn more about your offers: Home, Services, Case Studies, Book, Courses

- Discovery pages where your prospects can learn more about you or get in touch: About, Blog, Contact

Use this grouping to create two navigation menus, like this:

You can also use a different grouping, for example, public vs member access, with Log in – Sign up being your secondary navigation menu.

Advantages of splitting your navigation in two:

- Scannability: It's easier for your visitors to process two smaller groups of labels than one larger one.

- Your visitors feel less overwhelmed as they now have fewer labels to select from at once.

- Each label now has more chances of getting clicked (because of #2).

#97: How to make your copy more compelling by listening to your customers (and using Excel)

Once, I was writing new copy for a homepage of a business coach.

I asked her to send me all the testimonials she had. Then I created an Excel sheet with the following columns:

- **State before** to describe the state her prospects or their businesses were in before they reached out to her
- **Needs** to describe what they were looking for in terms of a solution to their problems
- **Reservations** to describe what made them hesitant to hire a business coach
- **Experience** to describe their experience of working with that business coach
- **State after** to describe how they felt afterwards

Next, I went through all the testimonials one by one and copy-pasted phrases from them into the corresponding columns.

Like this:

- **State before:** Lost, stuck and anxious / no one to help / tired of unpredictability / no clear direction / overwhelmed
- **Need:** Stable income / sustainable business / less hustle

You get the point.

And then, I just used the exact same phrases to create a smooth conversation that signals to the prospects that:

- what that business coach offers is what they're looking for

- she understands their problems
- she knows what they want to achieve

... while countering the reservations and offering social proof.

Like this:

"Feeling <u>stuck</u> and alone with your business struggles? <u>Overwhelmed</u> and <u>lacking direction</u>? I'll teach you how to run a <u>sustainable business</u> and earn a <u>stable income</u> with <u>less hustle</u>."*

* – underlined words copy-pasted from the Excel sheet.

Now, when her prospects read the exact same words they're already thinking to themselves, they'll feel like they've met an old friend who understands them.

And you'd rather hire a friend than a stranger, amiright?

To paraphrase Joanna Wiebe, a world-famous conversion copywriter and the founder of Copyhackers:

The most compelling copy doesn't sit inside your head. Or in the head of a copywriter you hire. It's in the hearts and minds of your customers. Your job is to lure it out, listen and repeat it back in persuasive ways.

#98: Should you use "we" (meaning you and your prospects) in your copy?

We all want to work less.

What a great phrase! It immediately shows your prospects that you're in the same boat and that you understand their problems.

Right?

Well...

When it comes to having vs solving problems, you can't put yourself on the same level as your prospects. Because if you claim you can solve those problems, how come you still have them yourself?

You're supposed to be ahead of them. Their leader. Their teacher. Their coach. Not their peer who's struggling with the same things.

So, in this case, you shouldn't use "we" when describing problems in the sales copy but instead address your prospects directly with "you":

- We are all worried about our business => Worried your new business will fail? [Do this to get this benefit]

- We all want to work less => You put in endless hours feeling guilty when you take a break, but you know it can't go on forever

Yet, you can use "we" – meaning both you and your prospects – when describing the process of working together. This signals to your prospects that once you take on their project, you'll be working as a team and helps them envision what working with you will be like.

#99: How to earn more from your most profitable audience segment

Let's say your target audience is ABCD, but people who end up buying / hiring you most are from an audience segment D.

Should you do anything different on your homepage?

On the one hand, you don't want to alienate the ABC people.

But, on the other, the Ds really want to give you their money.

Solution: Create a 'special corner' on your homepage just for the Ds.

Not in the header where you should keep your value proposition focused on your target audience in general.

Not in the next section where you may want to talk about yourself, your services or your product categories.

BUT dedicate the next section after that to your favorite audience segment and things they love, making sure it stands out from the rest.

Used lots of text before? Make that section as a background image and little text.

Too many images in the previous sections? Change the color or use fewer colors / visuals.

Examples:

- Small ecommerce shops can't get enough of your copy? Include a case study for your latest project for a small business just like that.

- You sell tableware, but it's the mugs with cats that are flying off the shelves? Add a section to your homepage presenting your best purr-sible cat mugs.

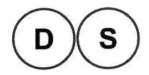

#100: When you shouldn't fix the issues on your website

What? It makes total sense to celebrate the 100th chapter of this book by telling you not to fix your website.

Yes, really.

Even if you are aware of some issues on your website, you shouldn't always fix them.

Don't touch your website if:

- You love the clients it gets you
- It's bringing in good money
- You don't cringe when you look at it

But if you hate your clients, want to earn more and / or are embarrassed by your website, act you must.

Assuming the amount of traffic isn't an issue, start with your main pain point.

Is it the clients?

Try:

- Making your value proposition / copy clearer and more focused on your favorite clients
- Changing the tone of your copy
- Including testimonials / case studies from the types of clients you want to attract more of

Also, check where your visitors come from. Maybe your website is fine, and you've just got a bunch of vegetarians judging your steakhouse.

Is it the money?

Try:

- Increasing your rates and polishing your sales pages to make it clear what value you deliver
- Looking at session replays to uncover other problems
- Looking at your competition to see if your target audience expects better web design

Is it your cringing?

Change whatever it is that makes you cringe (obviously), but make sure not to break anything in the process by asking yourself these questions:

- What did my visitors come to this page for?
- Will this new element interfere with my visitors' intentions?
- Can they easily read everything?
- Is my message still clear?
- Am I pulling my visitors' attention in a wrong direction?

Your next steps

Snackable tips are fun and all that, but wouldn't it be nice to have a coherent plan to follow to write a killer homepage, an effective sales page, or to discover everything that you still need to do on your website to make it successful?

Below, I've listed three checklists that have proved to be very helpful to both new and experienced business owners to do just that. You'll find them on this page on my website: **gillandrews.com/next-steps.**

- **"The" Website Content Checklist:** Agonizing over your web content? Use this checklist to know what to write (and how) on every important page of your website.

- **Ultimate Website Checklist**: All the features of a successful website at one glance.

- **Freelancer Homepage Checklist**: Turn your visitors into paying clients.

About the author

Gill Andrews is a copywriter and web consultant who helps small and medium business owners turn their underperforming websites into slick lead-generating machines.

When she's not busy reviewing websites and writing copy, she blogs on her own website **Gillandrews.com** about the problems she uncovers during her work with clients.

Have questions about the tips in this book? Want to stay in touch?

Email Gill at contact@gillandrews.com or follow her on LinkedIn or Twitter (@storieswithgill).

Index

Made in the USA
San Bernardino, CA
31 May 2020